# Dead Ringers

## Why Miners March

### Buried Truth from the Mountains

Edited and compiled by Wess Harris

APPALACHIAN
COMMUNITY
SERVICES

*A portion of the proceeds from the sale of this volume will be used to preserve the Whipple Company Store and the stories it has to tell.*

# DEAD RINGERS

## Why Miners March

### Buried Truth from the Mountains

Compiled and Edited by Wess Harris

Cover Design,
Front Photo Art,
& Book Layout
by Tom Rhule
Charleston, WV

**ISBN:** 978-0-9764706-9-4

**Appalachian Community Services**
229 Birtrice Road
Gay, West Virginia 25244

Printed in the USA on recycled paper, by the Employee Owners of Thomson-Shore in Dexter, Michigan.

# Content

# Acknowledgements

This customary and obligatory page offers opportunity to thank those who have made a work possible while absolving them of any blame for errors of the editor. Consider it done. Some special gratitude needs to be shown to two groups whose work does not physically appear herein.

In recent years countless miners and descendents of miners have offered stories and documents that supplement and confirm the tales in both *When Miners March* and this small volume. In addition to purely substantive contributions, their encouragement has been invaluable on those days when the tasks have seemed too great. Dwight Siemiaczko is a relentless researcher of all things Paint Creek. Kathryn Bowles offered her great grandfather Bill Derenge's autobiography. Terri Whitlock, granddaughter of Clarence E. "Red" Jones, provided the "smoking gun" that confirmed Van Bittner's sellout of the Union contracts. Elwood Maples saved documents that would have been lost forever —as well as the stories they tell! J.W. Sheets II stepped up and shared his grandfather's treasure that future generations can see as well as read their history. Joy and Chuck Lynn heard the bell ringing at the Whipple Company Store and protected the stories it has to tell. Cecil Roberts, President of the UMWA, has been an inspiration and his staff most supportive. They have always advocated for quality scholarship first and foremost. A sincere and humble thanks to all!

Secondly, unlikely and somewhat unwelcome heroes can be found at Radford University. Radford has agreed not only to house but also actively manage the William C. Blizzard/*When Miners March* collection. Much of the primary source material for both *When Miners March* and this work can now be accessed at the Radford University archives. Candidly, this is most unfortunate. These materials should ideally be kept within the state of West Virginia but that is not possible. Not one of the three institutions in West Virginia that might reasonably be expected to have the physical capabilities to house and preserve this incredible collection has the academic integrity to be trusted to tell the miners' tale and make it available to future generations. Sad but true. Researchers wishing to continue primary source research are directed to Radford. Special thanks to Theresa Burriss, Steve Helm, Gene Hyde, and Bill Kovarik. Many thanks to those who so richly deserve it, especially those who have gone on after lighting the way.

Shame on those who made this book necessary.

## Advice to Would-Be Poets

Away with pious references
To patriotism and to prayer,
As the naked child is born,
Let the truth lie cold and bare!

If there is a thing to tell
Make it brief and write it plain.
Words were meant to shed a light,
Not to cover it up again!

Don West, 1950

*...Sound advice for historians as well.*

# Introduction

This work is best viewed as a companion to William C. Blizzard's *When Miners March*. Matters cussed and discussed revolve around the history of our Union and the people who built it. The coal miners of West Virginia are central to the tale and yet the tale is much larger indeed. It is the story of America and her people. Who are we? Who have we been? Who will we become? Who decides?

The publication of this anthology is a declaration of our intention to reclaim the arena of Public History in the State of West Virginia, where the moneyed One Percent now controls most of the State's historic preservation resources. High salaried bureaucrats with an eye toward advancing their own careers shape the official interpretation and public perception of our past. Avoiding the wrath of King Coal takes precedence over quality scholarship in blatantly false and biased exhibits at our State Museum in Charleston, standard text books, and in classrooms taught by teachers all too often ignorant of their own past —or simply prohibited from teaching what they do know. In the suffocating climate of King Coal politics, the industry point of view has held sway for generations and nothing which might be seen as displeasing to the King is even entertained by those in charge of our cultural and educational institutions.

We offer this small volume not as a magnum opus on the men and women of the coal fields but as a catalyst to stimulate thought, discussion, and action regarding historical research and the sharing—teaching—of history. And *herstory*. It is often noted that the "winners" get to dictate the record of our past. It is equally true that despite a massive effort to spin the tale to the contrary, the writers in this collection refuse to accept defeat. Indeed, we believe that an honest look at events through the lens of the decades reveals a past in which we find "a lot of the little things the great people did, and a lot of the great things the little people did." (*When Miners March*, p. 382) While we place absolute priority on scholarly accuracy, no attempt is made to match the dry style of learned journals. "This is a people's history, and if it brawls a little, and brags a little, and is angry more than a little, well, the people in this book were that way, and so are their descendants." (*WMM*, p. 381–2)

New ground is broken here with a fresh look at the events of Blair Mountain and the infamous "treason" trials. Incredible stories from the Whipple Company Store change much of what we thought we knew about the early coal camps. A long buried 1963 look at John L. Lewis reveals a complexity oft ignored by scholars of both the left and the right. We also offer glimpses into the unions of the coal operators which tend to self–identify as associations or organizations rather than reveal their true nature: they are unions. In an age when Unions and labor history are at best on the fringes of the mainstream, can it be possible that a rather well-known carpenter's teachings would call us to carry a Union card?

In the spirit of searching for truth, we ask you, our readers, to join us in this commitment to take back our history and cultural institutions now in the service of King Coal. We invite public officials and historians charged with preserving and interpreting the history of our people to join us in this commitment. Together we can lift the dark veil smothering the truth, authenticity, and humanity of our past. We hope these pages offer a model for researching living and credible primary resources which for too long have been cloaked in fear and silence in "dead ringer" coalfield communities. It is time to speak truth to power. It is time to speak truth to our children. Come to life. Ring the bell.        —*Wess*

# Esau in the Coal Fields: Owing Our Souls to the Company Store
Michael Kline

Originally published in *Appalachian Heritage* (Volume 59, No. 5, Summer 2011.)

Emile Zola writing of working conditions in the French coal fields of the late nineteenth century penned vivid pictures of coal camp life which resonated deeply with mining developments in the new State of West Virginia during the same period. This fiction, based on Zola's six months of intensive research living and taking careful notes in the coal mining district of Borinage in the Alsace Region of northern France, featured such familiar themes as child labor, appalling working conditions, hunger, ever mounting debt at the company store, crippling and maiming from industrial accidents, and early death from industrial diseases. In *Germinal*, Zola explored another mortifying interaction between the company store and the village women and girls, daughters and wives of the coal miners: "It was a known fact that when a miner wished to prolong his credit, he had only to send his daughter or his wife, plain or pretty, it mattered not, provided they were complaisant." (p. 70)

In West Virginia we have our own versions of child labor, appalling working conditions, hunger, ever mounting debt at the company store, mine guards, Gatlin guns, and labor wars. But until quite recently, the use of female flesh to extend credit to feed the family was never mentioned by our own regional historians. We've pretty well accepted that early coal operators were a mean, iron–

willed breed bent on ruthless control and rising profits —
but surely not that mean.

Zola's *Germinal* was published in 1885. A year or
two later the young Collins brothers arrived in the
Fayette–Raleigh coal fields of southern West Virginia
from their home in Alabama, where Justus Collins had
gotten his start in personnel management overseeing
prison labor in the mines around Birmingham. These
young adventuring capitalists soon bought into thousands
of acres of rich coal lands just as the new industry was
emerging in the raw and lawless wilderness of our state.
So successful was Justus Collins in this land of
opportunity that in just a few years he had built and was
operating three, octagonal, turreted company stores in
southern Fayette County, the Justice Colliery Company
Store in Glen Jean, the Collins Colliery Company Store in
Prudence and the Whipple Colliery Company Store, at the
intersection of Rt. 612 near Oak Hill, West Virginia.
These stores serviced the needs of families employed at
the various Collins mines. The store at Glen Jean burned
to the ground in 1934, the year of Collins's death. The
same fate befell the Prudence store a few years later. But
the Whipple Store, completed in 1893, has miraculously
survived for nearly 120 years, a kind of social/industrial
history vault in which many unspeakable secrets are
stored.

This past July 4, my wife Carrie Kline and I had a
pre-arranged date with Joy and Chuck Lynn, owners and
interpreters of the Whipple Company Store Museum and
Learning Center these past five years. They bought the
imposing old building when it was on the verge of being

condemned and razed. Recently retired from business in Florida, they were attracted to the aging structure because of all the history which has been lived within its walls for more than a century.

Joy and Chuck agreed to take us on a tour of the building, even to show us the old embalming room in the basement which was in constant use from when the store was completed in 1893 until the federal government instituted the death certificate in 1932. We recorded their compelling interpretations, moving from one room to another throughout the long day. Our conversations began on the high, arched porch overlooking the parking area and roadways below.

The initial glaring question, of course, was why would two people entering their retirement years want to take on the colossal task of restoring and preserving this relic of the gilded era of coal company dominance. The more than 6000 square foot structure is in desperate need of a new roof, for starters, and of course, heating, and plumbing. The list of needed repairs is formidable. Joy Lynn explained that taking on the company store was more to her than just a passing fancy.

**Joy Lynn**: "My mother is a coal miner's daughter, and my grandmother is coal mining family all the way back to the beginning. Mother was raised nearby on the New River in Brooklyn. I was born in Oak Hill Hospital just two miles up the road and Granny has been here all her life. Mother has been back and forth between Brooklyn and Michigan. I guess this is really a rescue project. The roof is in bad shape. But with the amount of history surrounding this building, tearing it down was something I didn't want to see happen. Restoring it as a museum was a project we wanted to take on."

The Whipple Company Store was completed a couple of decades into the burgeoning coal and timber rush in the wake of the American Civil War. Soldiers from invading armies of the North had gone back home after the War with tales of the huge trees and rich outcroppings of coal. Surveyors and engineers soon came for a closer look.

For a clearer sense of how this land and resources grab played out in Fayette County and beyond, I reread Ron Eller's *Miners, Millhands and Mountaineers: Industrialization of the Appalachian South, 1880 – 1930* (1982). The fine-toothed precision of Eller's research makes for troubling reading. The chaos and looting of the region's natural wealth and environmental splendor was akin to the feverish activity of mad dogs in the sheep with blood on their fangs. The new social order that rose to power between 1880 and 1930 quickly abbreviated the United States Bill of Rights in industrial communities which they built and controlled, and took care of business with ruthless, self-proclaimed authority. In many coal and timber producing counties, venture capitalists with small armies of mine guards built their own courthouse towns— and courthouses—to baffle existing systems of law and order. Controlling the assessor's office and county land records were essential steps in the ever-expanding development of mills, mines, and railroads.

The vast influx of outside wealth in the 1880s and 1890s financed the passing of an old pre-Civil War order rooted in the rawness of the frontier, a well-defined local power structure dating to the times of earliest settlement. Now, an invasive species of colonizers was having its way with local traditions of leadership and displacing a diverse, agrarian, largely bartering economy with rail transportation, industrial wages, Gatling guns, and a cash economy conducted through the company store.

Suddenly the remote vastness of the southern Appalachians was buzzing with new industrial enterprise as European immigrants fresh from Ellis Island flooded into boom towns and labor camps to join contract labor from the cotton fields of Alabama and local men and boys from hard scrabble farms scattered throughout the hollows and hillsides of the region.

**Chuck Lynn**: "The men coming here from Ellis Island, of course, [were] getting caught up in the system before they arrived. They got a train trip from Ellis Island down to here and were in debt to the company the minute they stepped off the train. Of course they'd be paid in company store scrip. They'd never have cash to send for their families overseas.

"The company would provide the new arrivals with  carbide lamps and tools needed to start work. During the Depression immigrants were hoping to get work in their field if they were stone cutters or in the laboring trades. So they get off the boat and there's somebody saying, 'We'll give you a trip to where there are plenty of jobs and good living conditions and —oh, there's just a few catches along the way.'

"On election day the people who collected the ballots in most cases around here, were the mine bosses. So the bosses handed out a ballot already filled out and ready to sign. If the miners didn't sign it they would lose their jobs and get thrown into the streets. That's how the bosses kept all the politicians under control."

Construction of railroads penetrated the bountiful commons of the Appalachians to coincide with the opening of mines and lumber mills. In Fayette County coal and timber development followed the Chesapeake and Ohio Railway, completed through the New River Gorge in 1873. Coal mining companies could timber up a heading and open a mine for very little investment. Before they could go to work shooting and loading coal, miners were impelled to build the infrastructure which made possible the removal of coal from underground, placing timbers and laying track without pay. They had to buy the tools with which to mine the coal. They were paid only for the coal they loaded—and the company did the weighing.

But even with all this easy access to untold fortunes and totalitarian control of their workers, the coal operators feared unions and unionizing activities in adjoining states and beyond. After the economic slump of 1893, the nonunion coal fields of West Virginia emerged on the national coal market with a decided edge over Ohio and Pennsylvania dogged with labor troubles and crippling strikes. Production rose astronomically in West Virginia over the next few decades as the state's natural wealth was hauled away to the Great Lakes region and beyond in coal trains that always came back empty.

The Whipple Company Store has maintained an iconic connection with that era for almost 120 years. It is a flash point for local memory. And the man who built it, Justus Collins, driven by fears of organized labor, was determined to keep the union out of southern Fayette County. Forever. With that in mind he designed the store primarily as a fortress and staffed it with armed operatives posing as clerks and spying on customers while filling their orders from shelves behind the glass counters.

**Joy Lynn**: "He called it the Whipple Colliery Company Store. Whipple was his wife's family name. She was Lucy Whipple Dent Collins [with Georgia roots] and their daughter was Amy Whipple Collins.

"Justus Collins designed his company store as a security system. It wasn't built for beauty. It was built so the company owners and the company store workers could hear and see everything. Back then the only form of security people had was the guns they were toting, and their eyes and ears. Justus Collins brought the Baldwin-Felts men here from Bluefield and from the coal mining companies that he owned near Pocahontas."

Lon Savage, author of *Thunder in the Mountains*: The West Virginia Mine Wars 1920–21 (1990), reports in The West Virginia Encyclopedia that

"The Baldwin-Felts Detective Agency played a controversial role in the early years of the coal industry of southern West Virginia, enforcing public law at the direction of coal operators who hired them. Their often brutal, repressive policies, especially toward union miners, contributed significantly to the violence of the period. From the beginning, Baldwin-Felts agents were deputized by hard-pressed local sheriffs to maintain law and order, but coal operators increasingly used them to prevent organization of the miners by the United Mine Workers of America. The guards kept union sympathizers from entering the coal camps. They spied on miners, reporting those with union sympathies, their highly organized spy system extending even into the UMWA leadership. In 1902 they helped break a strike in the New River Field. Eventually, their overriding purpose in West Virginia was to prevent unionization of the miners."

**Joy Lynn**: "Those men could stand hidden behind the bases of the arch on both sides of the front porch, stand there with guns, look in the windows opposite, and look out into the road in front of the company store. So the windows were strategically placed for that reason. The original wooden steps were very steep and narrow, no hand rails."

The steep and narrow access would have made it difficult for more than a couple of men to rush the building at one time. Armed to the teeth, the guards were strategically placed to handle whatever threats the workers might pose in the heat of strikes or other disputes. The Whipple Store was a no-nonsense, state-of-the-art design for labor management at every imaginable level. It was a metaphor for the owner's resolve to keep the union out. It was fortified to protect the interests of an occupying owner class, and its staff of mine guards was capable of unleashing well directed armed force from within if ever it became necessary to do so.

**Joy Lynn**: "So they who came in and out. Women were primarily the shoppers in the company store. They actually enjoyed themselves and could converse with one another."

Joy recalls how eager her family was to get the store open as a museum and learning center after they acquired it in 2006. At the time of the opening in May 2007, the last whispers of local memory about the fragile old structure were still audible.

**Joy Lynn**: "We decided to open in spite of the condition of the building because most of the people who could give us any history would be in their late seventies, eighties and nineties. We've already had quite a number of people who lived this history come back here as visitors to the building. They've been giving us specific stories about their experiences here. I try to write people's comments after every tour so I can get as much of it documented as possible."

With her round, open face and friendly brown eyes, Joy Lynn invites confidences and sharing. Like Kanzeon, the Buddhist incarnation of compassion, she hears the cries and painful recollections of a troubled region. As a recipient of so many memories and testimonials, Joy explains her system for evaluating what she hears.

**Joy Lynn**: "Older people from surrounding communities come in here to tell me what I don't know. They often think that because I'm 'just a young girl' I can't possibly know anything about this, because they've lived it. When they tell me their stories, they get a dot on the wall and they get their story written down. When I have three dots I tell the story to others."

By triangulating what she hears, Joy has been able to develop an interpretation for the museum based on details that bubble up from her conversations with local visitors. These revelations are always stunning—often painful, and as a curator of local memory she is respectful of what she hears.

**Joy Lynn**: "We have had people coming in here whose mothers had to go through very hard times to raise them. They don't want that publicized. Some of the things are humiliating. And they made these sacrifices because they nurtured and cared about one another. They lived in these small communities by themselves and were governed by coal owners. People talk about how awful it was, but many people come in and tell stories about how life was so good. They cared about one another. They loved one another. They watched each others' backs."

The Whipple Company Store sold everything from canned goods, clothing, and crowbars—to live canaries. The birds were sold in little wooden cages and accompanied the miners to their work places underground. The tiny lungs were fatally affected by poisonous gasses, and the bird's sudden death warned the miners of the presence of odorless "black damp" in the underground room.

The old freight room's entrance is to the left of the porch and its floor-to-ceiling shelves are full of mining memorabilia. Some of the items were left behind with little interpretive information after the store closed in 1954, and it has been the Lynns's quest to learn from local visitors about the terminology and function of some mining equipment from earlier times. Some details that are hard to hear. Joy points to a small aluminum dinner pail on a nearby shelf.

**Joy Lynn**: "This little mining bucket here we just had a recent story on. I didn't know anything about the dinner bucket. I called it a little kid's picnic bucket. A gentleman came in last year with his grown children and grandchildren. He had been a miner for 50–some years. With his family members crowding around, he was telling them about all this equipment, and the canary story, and about the mine boss, and the children going in the mines. He finally turns to me, points to that dinner bucket, and he pokes me in the arm and he says, 'Little lady, tell me about that bucket.' I says, 'Well, sir, I don't know anything about that bucket.'

"He says, 'When you lived in the coal camps back early on, if your daddy got killed in the mines, your mama had to pack up and leave. There was no ifs, ands or buts. She was out, out, just out. But if she had a young boy eight or older, he could mine in place of his daddy, and that way his mama could stay in the mining camp.' The old gentleman went on to explain how you'd give the children eight to twelve years old those smaller dinner buckets to keep with them at all times. That way the men who were more seasoned miners would be alerted to a young boy that might need some help. Or if they needed their back watched in the mines, maybe that young miner wasn't the right person to choose. Those boys tagged along behind men who might educate them.

"So I told him, I said, 'Sir, that's a great story, but I've never seen any documentation about smaller sized dinner buckets. I haven't seen them in photographs.'

"And he says, 'I can show you my dinner bucket, because I went in and mined for my mama when I was nine years old. Happiest day of my life was when I turned thirteen and all the men on my shift bought me my man bucket. And I still have both of them.'

"A man and woman came in yesterday, and she told me, 'That dinner bucket story's true. There's a lady that lived four doors from us and said her little nine year-old boy was in the coal mines.' So a child working down in the mine was doing his daddy's work.

"Their dinner buckets, of course, were very important pieces of mining equipment. Most of the historic photographs of old coal miners show them holding their dinner buckets. We explain about what it meant when a miner poured his fresh water out on the ground. A lot of men who went into the shafts had safety issues about conditions underground, and when they couldn't get the ear of a mine boss or somebody to pay attention to their complaint, they would pour their water out, and all the men would walk out of the mines. That was always a signal, water poured out of their canteen meant that no one goes back in the mines until the problems are resolved. Saved a lot of lives that way."

In the center of the stock room is a six by eight foot freight elevator, hand powered with a thick rope that passes around a large iron pulley wheel at the top of the sixty foot shaft.

**Joy Lynn**: "We use it for everything from the basement to the ball room. It's still 100 percent functional. This elevator seats firmly into the basement floor downstairs, and the double doors on the west side of the building open up. Any kind of pony carts or trucks could back into the area down there and unload onto the elevator. They would bring their merchandise up to this floor to be [inventoried] and put into the company store.

"The elevator would then continue up to this little secret second floor, which doesn't look like much more than a closet. It's about five feet tall and you would unload back this way over our heads. Coffins would've been stored up in that area until 1932. They didn't want women to see anything like that. They needed coffins every day, because we lost mining men in numbers to mine accidents, and occupational diseases. And the coffins would service three mines in the area. Some days they'd need forty, some days they'd need ten, some days one, and some days sixty. We're talking about the period between 1893 and 1930."

The final upward destination of the elevator is the third floor ballroom which provides rare insights into the social lives of the new owning class in Fayette County in the 1890s.

**Joy Lynn**: "The ballroom on the third floor is my favorite space, Justus and Lucy's ballroom. What you're seeing is the original 1893 room. Lucy chose gold colors from the West Virginia state flag to accentuate her lavender gown. The door [off the front side of the ballroom] is Lucy's 'ballroom adornment room.' The ladies would go in there and they would fix their hair or maybe their boot and garter. The room with the white door was where the men withdrew for a last smoke before they came out to dance. These men were coal owners and they would meet here because they didn't want people to know what they were doing. [With the threat of violence everywhere in the region], coal owners had to stay kind of in the background.

"Organ music would begin to play as men and women would come greet one another in the center of the dance floor. These elite dancers preferred waltzes. Ballroom floors were often suspended back in the 1800s because a slightly bouncy floor put a bounce into the step of the dancers."

The design also gave Collins and his detectives an acoustic structure for the surveillance of all spoken conversations in the store downstairs.

This level of control by the company men reached into every nook and cranny of the miners' lives. The threat of terror and level of fear in the daily lives of coal camp residents was palpable. Civil rights were unheard of. For more details on the kinds of challenges these conditions posed for union organizing, I turned again to W. C. Blizzard's *When Miners March*, edited by Wess Harris and based on firsthand accounts of the labor wars, especially the Battle of Blair Mountain, which rocked the West Virginia coal fields into the 1920s. Fayette, along with other southern coal mining counties, was repeatedly under Marshall Law. The ever vigilant company operatives were always on the watch for union organizers.

**Chuck Lynn**: "The Baldwin-Felts guards were not all carrying guns. Some of them were miners. Some of them were local law officials, sheriffs on the company payroll. So any talk of unionizing would be nipped in the bud. The men would be immediately fired."

**Joy Lynn**: "We don't have any pictures of the inside of this building. We have one of an inside picture of Justus Collins's twin store over in Glen Jean. It burned in 1934. It shows us this counter which is one of the most important features of this building. It is architecturally [designed as] a security system. This gentleman is a Baldwin-Felts detective. He posed as a clerk. Women were primarily the ones with information about the union meetings, because they were the ones here shopping and visiting with one another."

But with the acoustic design of the ceiling, even low level conversations bounce off the concrete walkway to the ceiling and back to the center of the store.

**Joy Lynn**: "This guy behind the counter can hear you. No matter where you are."

In the gilded age of the mining industry, companies recruited a diversity of workers from many parts of Europe, the agricultural fields of the deep South, as well as the surrounding hills and hollows of the mountain region. Justus Collins was a pacesetter in hiring a diverse labor force. Historian Ken Sullivan wrote:

"Collins's comment that mine managers should strive for a 'judicious mixture' of races and nationality groups, on the theory that diversity hampered unionization, is often quoted."

**Joy Lynn**: "Justus Collins had them all segregated in such a way so that they couldn't communicate with one another. If you came here and talked a foreign language, and you lived with the foreign language-speaking people, how're you going to learn English? You don't. So you can't understand; you can't band together; you can't unionize.

"The black people [experienced] intense segregation. Before the union came in, black people in Whipple lived directly behind the store, where soot [from passing C&O locomotives] would come down on them. The white people lived up above, and they had the white school. [In order to get to their own school each morning], the black children would have to cross paths at the white children's school and of course get beat up on a daily basis. We've had black people come in and tell us that.

"Blacks weren't allowed in the company store except at certain times on certain days. They had a window on the side of the building. They would hand their list in. The clerk would take care of everything and then hand it back out the window. Only certain days and times they were allowed in here.

"Everyone was kept separate. 'Hunk Hill' was across the street. Anybody who didn't speak the language was a 'hunky.' It didn't matter what nationality you were, German or Polish, Czechoslovakian, Hungarian or Italian. Those are mainly what we had here. And there were many single men coming from Ellis Island, no family, nobody. They'd stick those men into more dangerous areas underground. Nobody was accounting for these people.

"And when you hear the stories about how the miners were expendable and mules were more important than the men, it was because the men didn't cost anything. But those mules were expensive to replace."

A little later on in the afternoon, we fumbled down a long, dark stairway into the basement where Chuck Lynn joined us for a closer look at the dark underbelly of the Whipple Store.

**Chuck Lynn**: "This room here was the embalming room, a room inside the basement, but with windows. So it's a straight pass through rather than bringing bodies in through the front door. The embalming service was in operation up through 1931. The miners' burial fund was a deduction from their check. If they didn't have their burial fund up to date or were a newly started employee, then the cost of their coffin would have been deducted from their last pay check before the family would get anything. This is where they would have dealt with the bodies of miners who died anywhere in the coal camp. I imagine there were several bodies handled through here from uprisings or any mine wars. There are many unmarked cemeteries around here where the bodies would have gone."

**Carrie Kline.** "What did you mean uprisings and mine wars?"

**Chuck Lynn**: "The many mine wars: Paint Creek, Cabin Creek and of course Blair Mountain where the mine workers retaliated against the mine owners. They would go on strike. They would be thrown out of their company housing and forced to live in tents until they came to terms with the company. A lot of times they didn't, and of course the company would bring in other workers to substitute for them, other "scab" workers, they would call them in the union field, to live in their houses and work their jobs for the same, or even lower, wages than they were being paid. Pretty rough life. But if you abided by the rules, put up with the situation and pay, you did fine.

"The Paint Creek Strike [of 1913] came up as far as Dothan just up the road from here. And a lot of union miners from here marched on Blair Mountain in 1921 because this was all union territory at the time. But then again, it wasn't a strong union. The coal owners could decide whether to abide by union demands, or just completely ignore them."

The rapidly expanding coal and timber economies, well oiled with state and federal subsidies and other tax breaks, made their own rules. They built their own towns with company schools and churches. The coal camps and work places were patrolled by company guards. Free assembly of the workers was strictly forbidden. The company doctor saw the workers, heard their complaints, and told them to go back to work. The companies called the shots, maintained their own police forces, even minted the coins with which they paid their workers. The "scrip" they issued was good only at the company store. The store itself was a fortress constructed to buttress company control against possible infiltration by union organizers and ideas of collective bargaining. Such total control by a few at the top flies in the face of American democratic ideals as guaranteed in the Bill of Rights for every citizen. Throughout the coal mining industry and its communities of workers at the time the Whipple Store was built in the early 1890s, a system of serfdom and wage slavery was already well established. But humiliation went even deeper.

Just off the ballroom on the third floor of the Store is a smaller room toward the back of the building. In early photographs it's the only curtained room. It served as a fitting room, so it has been frequently told, where women were accompanied by one of the guards from the first floor to try on shoes they had seen displayed in the shoe department. A woman, of course, seldom had money of her own, and barely enough scrip or credit at the company store to cover the week's groceries and rent. So when she got up to the shoe room she found it furnished with a cot upon which the guard encouraged her to sit while trying on the shoes. When the door shut behind her, she found herself alone with the guard.

**Joy Lynn**: "Over the past several years we've had eight or ten women refer to this as "the rape room." After they got their lovely shoes they would have to pay for them in this room. Then they would be escorted back downstairs to resume their shopping, or pick up their children down there, or what have you. They would have to keep their mouths shut tight about what had happened to them upstairs. If the miners would get wind of this, what would a husband do? How would he react? First thing he would do is react, most men. But if the men were belligerent, they'd soon have 'accidents' in the mines, and we've had reports of that as well. So the women had to do what they had to do and keep their mouths shut.

"One woman comes in and tells me a story. She says, 'I know about that shoe room, because Mama had to go into the shoe room once.' And she says, 'Mama wouldn't buy shoes any more after that. She wrapped her feet and made her own cardboard and newspaper shoes. And that's all she wore the whole time they lived in the camp.' The daughter was 82 years old who told me about her mama's shoes."

Three years ago Joy Lynn had an unexpected, eye-opening visit in the Company Store one day from a woman who had spent much of her professional life working in the bookkeeping office with access to the first floor safe.

**Joy Lynn**: "As she tells me her story of working for many years in this office she points out the wear of her own shoes on the floor. She describes stepping up to the door of the safe which was installed in 1907 by the New River Company. The man inside hands her two guns which she puts in the pockets of her apron. Then she goes to her desk where she spends the day keeping necessary records for coal miners, and she would meet them at the window, as her business required. The safe stored the book keeper's guns along with moonshine and liquor, tobacco, and rolling papers. It also housed morphine and other medications, pay envelopes, mining maps, as well as paper scrip over five dollars. She said this safe was where they would keep the paper scrip and, pointing to each shelf as she described its contents, she was explaining what everything was.

"And she suddenly pointed to five mysterious pieces of paper I had been storing on the shelf under glass and said, 'You've got Esau!' Now I didn't know what she was talking about, so I'm listening. I said, 'What is it?' And she said, 'You shouldn't have that. That shouldn't be here. You don't need to have that.' I said, 'Oh. Well can you tell me what it is?'

'Well,' she said, 'it was the way women were administered food.' I said, 'Oh, well how did they do that?' Because these little white company issued chits were dated 1922 through '25, '27, in that era. She said, 'Well, sometimes the men would get sick and couldn't mine coal, and the women would need to have food for their children. So the superintendent would administer this for them.' So I asked, 'How would the women pay that back?' They didn't have the ways and means to pay for much of anything. But they wouldn't let their children starve. 'You need to get rid of that,' she said again. 'I don't think you should have that in here. Let me take it.'

I said, 'No, that's OK. I'll take care of it. Let's go on and look at something else.' And later we got a few minutes alone on the porch. I said, 'You know, I'd really be interested in a little bit more information on how that paper scrip was administered and how the Esau was paid back.' She said, 'Well, you really don't want to keep that back there, because you might have some women come in here, and that will be upsetting to them.' I said, 'Well, I don't really understand why it would be so upsetting. Women make sacrifices all the time to feed their children. That's not so unusual.' She says, 'If a man could get back to work in the mines in 30 days, and he was a good miner, the woman wouldn't have to pay it back.'"

Though penniless and often with her family facing possible eviction, a miner's wife nonetheless possessed physical assets which the Baldwin-Felts guards and other company men at the store often found compelling and greatly desirable. Esau was a kind of super credit issued by the company store superintendent only to mothers of hungry children. The name of Esau comes from the sad story in Genesis, the Twenty–fifth Chapter, in which Esau, a starving hunter staggering into his brother's tent, begs his brother Jacob for a bowl of beans. Jacob feeds his brother, but only after forcing Esau to sign away his birthright.

For the miner's wife, forfeiting on the Esau agreement meant submitting to the sexual depredations of the company men, compromising her own integrity and birthright, all for a poke of beans to feed her children, or a week's rent to keep a roof over their heads. She perceived herself without options, totally victimized by a well-established, bureaucratic system conducted through the company store at a time when corporate profits were mushrooming: the black gold rush of the eastern mountains. But corporate ethics and responsibilities had yet—and still have yet to be defined outside the caldrons of raw profiteering. Such excesses were built on a system which kept the workers' pockets empty and their spirits broken, the starved-out circumstances in which Esau found himself when Jacob demanded his birthright in return for a bowl of beans.

That bureaucratized rape has been a feature of capitalist expansion and industrial development in the coal fields was a shocking revelation to me when I first heard about it fifteen years ago. A retired coal miner in eastern Ohio recorded for me childhood memories of a "Polish patch," a mining camp in the shadow of a huge tipple. He told me that after his Dad was injured in a slate fall underground, his mother had to go in person to the superintendent's office to make "other arrangements" when she could no longer pay the rent on their company house.

I still wonder how widely the term "Esau" has been used to describe this pervasive practice throughout the Gilded Age of West Virginia's beloved robber barons, for whom we have named our towns, colleges, churches, hospitals and banks, yes, especially banks, throughout the region. What has been the imprint of this totalitarian takeover of the past century and a half on our present social and environmental dilemmas? Would you think that a coal operator who would send an eight year old boy to work in his diseased father's place in an underground mine would hesitate to take advantage of the boy's mother? How does what our fore parents went through continue to hang upon our present generation a "company store" sense of ourselves? Old, established patterns of capitulating to company demands, selling ourselves short, even voting against our own best interests, have followed us into presently troubled times. This despondent pattern reflects the oppressive conditions over time of a one-industry economy owned and operated by and for the benefit of outside interests. It's a lot of baggage to carry, a dark image to try to shake off.

Even now we daily give up our birthright for a bowl of Esau beans: a minimum wage pay check at MacDonald's, a shift of dangerous work in the bowels of the earth, a bag of prescription pain pills, or very modest subsidies from our currently exploding oil and gas boom. Think about what our overlords have taken from us in return for these crumbs.

Much of the responsibility for these gulag conditions in West Virginia's early development lies with the many administrations of state and local government presiding over the past century and a half of extractive corporate management by outside interests. Our elected leadership has overseen the transfer of ownership of the region's natural wealth from local family deeds to foreign interests. Our leaders have always promoted our state as being "open for business" and upheld the excesses of the coal industry as models of bullish progress, a source of commerce and jobs, despite thousands of industrial deaths and degraded landscapes. Over the past century and more, many public officials charged with safeguarding the interests of their constituents, began instead rubbing shoulders with captains of the incipient coal industry, paving the way for out-of-state money men and free wheeling practices.

In *Miners, Millhands and Mountaineers*, Eller notes one memorable exception to the wholesale accommodation of wealthy entrepreneurs by willing public servants: an 1884 report by the West Virginia Tax Commission. This document warns local citizens that "non-residents are carrying off the most valuable resources of the state, threatening to leave West Virginia in the near future despoiled of her wealth and her resident population poor, helpless and despondent." The Commission concluded,

> *"The question is whether this vast wealth shall belong to persons who live here and who are permanently identified with the future of West Virginia, or whether it shall pass into the hands of persons who do not live here and who care nothing for our State except to pocket the treasures which lie buried in our hills."*

The warning of the tax commission went unheeded.

Faced with the grim realities of our industrialized past, many readers wince at these painful images of dubious stereotypes, of "radicals" and union organizers at war with state militias and the National Guard. And now, with the Lynns' remarkable documentary work at Whipple, a whole new sense about the victimization of women has come to light. So why should we mine the underbelly of West Virginia's agonizing past for these devilish details? Aren't some things better forgotten? Can't we just let bygones be bygones?

For more clarity on these issues I turned again to Lon Savage in *The Goldenseal Book of the West Virginia Mine Wars* (p.48) in an anniversary speech he gave at Matewan, West Virginia on May 19, 1989:

*". . . Let's tell everyone our history; let's brag about it; let's revel in it. Acknowledging and telling our history may even change the way we see ourselves. If the history of violence in Appalachian mining is ever to change, it will happen with an acknowledgement, a full airing, and an understanding of that history. . . Most importantly it will help us understand ourselves . . . more rapidly than almost anything else we can do."*

\*\*\*\*\*\*\*\*\*\*\*\*\*\*\*\*\*\*\*\*\*\*\*\*\*\*\*\*\*\*\*\*\*\*\*\*\*\*\*\*\*\*

## Epilogue

To wrap up the loose ends of this complex story in late May, Carrie Kline and I once again visited the Whipple Store to touch base with Joy and Chuck Lynn. They told us that, three days earlier, a man in his early nineties had visited the store. They showed him around the imposing porch, which he had known from his childhood. When they stepped inside the freight room, the man poked Joy on the shoulder, said, "Hey lady, did you ever hear of Esau? They got my mother with that Esau…"

\*\*\*\*\*\*\*\*\*\*\*\*\*\*\*\*\*\*\*\*\*\*\*\*\*\*\*\*\*\*\*\*\*\*\*\*\*\*\*\*\*\*\*

*"Whether a woman is raped at gunpoint or trafficked into sexual slavery by an occupying force, the sexual abuse will shape not just her own but her community's future for years to come.*

*"Survivors face emotional torment, psychological damage, physical injuries, disease, social ostracism and many other consequences that can devastate their lives."*

—Amnesty International

West Virginia Traditional Life

**Goldenseal**

January 10, 2011

Michael Kline
114 Boundary Avenue
Elkins, WV 26241

Dear Michael,

Thank you for your recent manuscript concerning the Whipple Store. I found it to be very interesting, though very challenging in certain respects. As we had discussed on the phone, our normal maximum manuscript length falls somewhere around 3,000 words. We are about double that here, I would estimate. Much of the wide-ranging industrial history in this manuscript could possibly be trimmed in favor of some additional specific details about the Whipple community and Whipple Colliery. But there are other, larger problems.

The main challenge we face from a publishing standpoint is the overall intent of this manuscript to expose the sins of the coal industry, accusing them of rape and murder on a grand scale. I'm not sure GOLDENSEAL is the right outlet for this sort of exposé. I don't take issue with or doubt the testimony of Joy and Chuck Lynn or their informants. As we discussed on the phone, I am even willing to address these sensitive issues in a special sidebar associated with a general history of the Whipple Store. The current manuscript, however, is very pointed in its intention and shows no quarter, not just with Whipple, but with the coal industry as a whole and with other capitalistic interests.

The history of West Virginia is painful at times, to be sure, and I don't shrink from my responsibility to address the tough parts in GOLDENSEAL as the occasion demands. Michael, I'm afraid this manuscript is simply beyond the pale when it comes to controversy. We cannot go to press with these industry-wide accusations of heinous behavior, especially without corroborating evidence or documentation.

I know you have put a lot of work into this story and have been anxious for a more positive response from me. I have read this story over twice, however, and don't see how it would fit in our pages. In the unlikely event that you would like to rework this story into something less provocative, I would be glad to help you in any way I can. Just let me know. In the meantime, I am returning your materials to you, with my regrets.

Sincerely,

John Lilly
Editor

JL:ca

Enclosures

West Virginia Division of Culture and History
The Cultural Center, 1900 Kanawha Boulevard East, Charleston, WV 25305-0300
304/558-0220  TDD 304/558-3562  FAX 304/558-2779

# Behind the Coal Curtain: Efforts to Publish the Esau Story in West Virginia
Michael Kline

I was tipped off about the Whipple Store by my friend, Wess Harris. For the past forty years I have been following local recollections of the early days of Union organizing through the coal fields of West Virginia and eastern Kentucky. With Carrie Kline, I have been a lifelong collector and singer of coal mining songs. I published an article about former United Mine Workers President Arnold Miller's memories growing up on Cabin Creek in the 1930s and '40s in Goldenseal's Book of Mine Wars, published by West Virginia's Department of Culture and History in 1991. Carrie Kline and I were asked by the Park Service Headquarters at Glen Jean to provide training in oral history gathering for their staff as they undertook a study of African-American mining culture and history in the New River Gorge. I have come at half a century of research in West Virginia by way of oral sources and have recorded hundreds of reflections and recollections of more than two generations of working people here.

West Virginia's official social history, especially as interpreted by the State Division of Culture and History in Charleston, has never entertained the possibility of Esau. Mainstream historians, including those specializing in Labor History, have never touched it, though it is a documented undercurrent of coal field lore and memories borne by some of our oldest neighbors and family members. Joy and Chuck Lynn, owners of the Whipple Company Store have not published nor publicized the story of Esau widely out of a respect for the emotions still raw among decedents of those involved in the system. They agreed to my article with some reservations and I hope these concerns have been honored.

I initially wrote Esau for Goldenseal Magazine, a folklife quarterly published by West Virginia's Division of Culture and History in Charleston. I have published a score of articles in Goldenseal over the past thirty-three years, and was anxious to reach those readers with this story. Through the development of the piece last fall and into the winter, I was in phone contact with the editor, John Lilly, an old friend of mine, about the emerging details, especially regarding Esau. I wanted him to know what was coming. And though he expressed nervousness about this revelation, nonetheless he encouraged me to finish and submit the manuscript by February 1. Sadly, he rejected my submission, because, as he explained, the piece "shows no quarter, not just with Whipple, but with the coal industry as a whole and with other capitalistic interests." I have since wondered when the coal industry became such a fragile flower that it should be somehow removed from scrutiny increasingly focused upon its dark and draconian past. I bet Mother Jones would have some choice words for John Lilly. The air would be blue.

Lilly's rejection letter is evidence of the sinister power of the coal industry then –and now –and its ability to intimidate well meaning public service workers such as John Lilly, along with judges, state legislators and anyone else who is in a position to protect the industry's image.

I sense the long shadow of Commissioner Randall Reid-Smith cast across the decision to suppress the Esau story. Reid-Smith has already made his Coal Industry loyalties abundantly clear. He serves at the will and pleasure of the governor.

The Lilly letter reminds me of that stifling feeling I first knew working in the coal fields as a community organizer in Johnson's War on Poverty in the mid-1960s. It was a sense of the isolation in which we were trying to generate programs for social change. We felt that nobody out there in mainstream U.S.A., especially the bureaucrats writing Poverty War legislation and programs, could possibly have the slightest idea of challenges facing coal field communities. In places where we worked there was a poverty of information coming in and going out, as though we had been left for dead. It was like a big brattice had been hung to shade out any light of understanding connecting us with the diverse social landscapes and economies defining much of the rest of the nation.

I remembered talk I heard as a child growing up in the Cold War era about human rights abuses in the Soviet Union. When the high-ranking leaders of the Communist Party during much of the Twentieth Century gained totalitarian control over the Russian people through stern measures to isolate them from other nations and ideas, we talked about human suffering going on "behind the Iron Curtain." It was a place, our leaders said, where ordinary people lived in fear and darkness.

As I discovered working for community self determination in the coal fields of the 1960s, the political leadership of our State had woven for us, from the time of our coal mining ancestors, a Coal Curtain, a mantel of darkness and devaluation. The rest of the world has very little idea about the symbiotic relationship among the Coal Industry, the courts, and the hallways of State Government in Charleston. Ironically, we have been taught by the coal barons to be suspicious of "outsiders," dating to our earliest Union organizing struggles. Isolation from the outside world and a fear of strangers: that's a mix which has all too often left us poor, destitute and robbed of our natural birthright, that is, our water, air, natural landscapes and the mineral wealth that lies beneath them. These treasures are ours, in common, by any fair standard of justice and democratic living and sharing. The blackout on news and censorship of historical truths behind this Coal Curtain today renders us who live here confused and largely powerless. A recently composed song echoes the refrain:

> *Well tell me now who is to blame,*
> *who shakes King Coal's hand?*
> *Who fails to protect us,*
> *and who sells out our land?*
> *It's the greedy politicians*
> *at the company's beck and call,*
> *From the judges up to the President,*
> *I would  blame them all*
> —Greg Artzner, *Magpie*

Living in this climate of supreme corporate control and influence buying, I feel this censorship keenly. We need to revitalize our labor history resources not just here in West Virginia, but all over the coal fields, as initiatives to strip us of our hard fought labor rights are gaining momentum. We need to teach younger workers what is at stake in keeping a tight grasp on our common history. Tune in to freedom movements springing up all over the globe in places where the authorities said it could never happen. They are great sources of inspiration. Everyone seems ready to throw off the yoke.

Michael Kline
Independent Folklorist
and Audio Producer
Elkins, West Virginia

**Saturday Gazette-Mail**

FEBRUARY 25, 2012   CHARLESTON, WEST VIRGINIA

## Smiles

To history buff Michael Kline of Elkins, who won a Plattner Award for Creative Nonfiction for his account of coal industry oppression once centered at the Whipple company store in Fayette County — and also won a state History Hero award with his wife.

# SCRIP POLICY IS ILLEGAL

## Says Mayor Dawson In Lashing Out Against Violation Of State Statute

Fayetteville, W. Va., Sept. 9- (Special)- Mayor Daniel Boone Dawson of Charleston, Republican candidate for Governor, in a statement issued here today lashed out at the illegal transfer of coal company scrip in violation of the state law which he declared had become prevalent in many southern West Virginia mining towns.

Mayor Dawson said that it had been brought to his attention some time ago that this evil had been working a hardship on both the miners and independent merchants. After an extensive study of the problem the Charleston Chief Executive declared that he was certain if not the letter of the law was being violated.

"The wholesale discounting and transferring of scrip is lowering the standard of living of the coal miners and creating an unwholesome atmosphere in the mining centers," asserted the Republican gubernatorial candidate. "In 1927 the scrip law was altered to prevent the trafficing in scrip. That law should be rigidly enforced and if necessary additional legislation enacted to make the transfer of scrip absolutely illegal."

Mayor Dawson said that he was of the opinion that additional legislation outlawing these practices may be necessary and that at a later time and after additional study he would further expand on this subject which be termed "vital to the interest of West Virginia miners and to the mining communities."

**THE TIMES-RECORD**
SPENCER, WEST VIRGINIA
*PUBLISHED IN 1940*

# West Virginia's Gilded History
Tom Rhule

Tom Rhule is an independent journalist, researcher, and blogger from Charleston, West Virginia. He has a reputation for finding stories that mainstream journalists have missed —or have chosen to avoid.

West Virginia's Golden Horseshoe Society is the longest running program of its kind in the United States. Since it began, more than 15,000 eighth graders have received the Golden Horseshoe Award in recognition of their knowledge of West Virginia history. Upon bestowing the accolade, the state ceremoniously inducts students as "knights" and "ladies" of the Golden Horseshoe Society.[1]

The WV Department of Education promotes the "Society" to develop good citizenship in students. A close examination of its origin reveals a concept of citizenship far removed from the democratic ideals of our nation.[2]

In an interview about the State Historic Preservation Officer's willingness to sacrifice the historic resource at Blair Mountain to the mountaintop removal industry, Chris Green, professor at Marshall University recently revealed, "I have students who were top-of-the-line Golden Horseshoe people who don't know about the mine wars..."[3]

Responding to a congressionally mandated study over twenty years ago, ten prominent historians re-commended Blair Mountain as a site worth preserving. Their stated reason was crystal clear: "West Virginia's labor history is part of a larger historical theme which illustrates the struggle for liberties promised in the Bill of Rights."[4]

West Virginia's mine wars erupted in 1912, then resumed in 1919 after World War I. During the mine wars State leaders, coal companies and their local newspapers all portrayed the uprising as sedition, then later downplayed it all as little more than a series of wage disputes. Despite efforts by politically appointed state education leaders and mercenary revisionist historians to to revise and minimize WV's sordid history, there still remains enough evidence to prove that in 1921 the mine workers marched to battle for their civil liberties —for freedom of speech and assembly, freedom from the industrial feudalism of company towns, and freedom from the terrorism inflicted by the operators' private military.[5]

Simply stated, the Battle of Blair Mountain was an attempt by citizens to liberate the southern coal fields of West Virginia. Those who marched weren't seditious rioters and bomb throwing Bolsheviks as they were being portrayed at the time; they were patriots bent on redeeming their state from a rule of terror.[6]

Although the WV Department of Education's official Golden Horseshoe Society webpage describes the program's originator as a noted historian, the state agency fails to do Phil Conley justice. Before starting the Golden Horseshoe Society (and being declared a "noted historian"), Conley was a Human Relations Officer for the Consolidated Coal Company, running a blurb sheet for a coalition of coal owners that called themselves *The West Virginia Publicity Commission*. In 1921 Conley became first managing director for the American Constitutional Association (ACA), an organization so close to the WV Department of Education that by May of '21 the two agencies literally shared the same office space.[7]

In *When Miners March*, author William C. Blizzard recognized the ACA as a pro-fascist outfit, further revealing "...(i)n order to secure a 'good press' and ...to continue a tight grip over governmental affairs in the Mountain State, a group of operators and public officials ...hand in glove, ...banded together to form the American Constitutional Association."[8]

Conley is on record as having told the Executive Committee of the ACA that its partnership with the schools would enable the organization to "reach the adults through the medium of the children." He also reported to his group that the ACA had the potential of influencing eleven thousand teachers, and then proceeded to do so directly from the offices of the WV Department of Education.[9]

Another ACA strategy was apparently to provide political cover for state leaders to permit the coal owners associations to pay their own corporate attorneys to prosecute miners *on behalf of the State,* then later bill taxpayers $125,000 for their prosecutorial services.[10]

In July of 1922 the *New York Times* featured Conley's propaganda guild aggressively defending what it admits was "the state mine guard system."

# MINE GUARD UPHELD BY WEST VIRGINIA

## State, Through Press Agent,

### Denies Stories of Lawlessness and Starvation.

West Virginia now has a press agent. An organization which calls itself the American Constitutional Association, with headquarters at Charleston. W. Va., in a statement issued here yesterday announced that it was out to "correct the false impression which prevails concerning our commonwealth."

Need for the propaganda work is emphasized by the association because "throughout the United States people are thinking that we are only partly civilized, that our government has fallen down, and that life is held very cheap." The association charges that persons are being paid for "consistently criticising the State of West Virginia," to scare away industries that threaten to leave other States to be near the fuel supply. "Obviously it pays well," it was added, "to keep the directors of large industrial concerns believing that West Virginia has continuous labor trouble, that the Government of the State has broken down, and that we have a hotbed of lawlessness."

In defense of the mine guard system, the association said:

"The one thing that has been emphasized more than any other by outsiders is the so-called deputy sheriff or mine guard system. One is led to believe that West Virginia originated and has a monopoly on an unique plan, and that all other States are so highly civilized that they would not tolerate anything like it. The facts are that the same system is used in New York, Pennsylvania, Colorado, and in every other industrial State. Why is this system such a horrible thing for West Virginia and of so much value to the industries of the other States?"

Deploring the many investigations of conditions and reports of starving miners, the statement concluded:

"We venture the opinion that among our 1,400,000 citizens there are less people needing assistance than can be found in a score of blocks in New York City."

The New York Times

Published: July 31, 1922

*The*

## American Constitutional Association

*Soon after the uprising at Blair Mountain, powerful coal owners and politicians banded together not just to keep coal laborers from collective bargaining, but to erase the sordid history of the state's complicity of upholding the coal industry policy of terrorizing the public.*

*While it is true that corporations in other states paid gun thugs to break strikes, other governors had never ordered printing presses destroyed or editors jailed.*

Promoting Conley's Golden Horseshoe Society, WV School Superintendent William C. Cook stated that for students to become WV's best citizens, they "…should have knowledge of the past and present status of the State in order to estimate its future possibilities." Unfortunately when granting extraction industry leaders the unfettered ability to distort or otherwise bury the historic record of their excesses, Cook neglected to predict the dire effect it would have on the future of the State's citizenry.[11]

Thanks to the combined efforts of State leaders and their coal industry backers to cover up the history of oppression throughout West Virginia, it may never be determined just how widely the Esau system was used to terrorize the families of struggling laborers.[12]

Human rights organizations have defined rape as a weapon of war, used effectively to isolate families and control entire communities. It has often been diagnosed as systemic where paternalistic societies have fallen under military rule. Leading up to West Virginia's mine wars, virtually all of West Virginia's southern coal camps were paternalistic, in many ways similar to pre-Civil War southern cotton plantations. Coal owners were successful in their oppression only through the widespread use of their brutal private military, operating for years under the full consent of the State.[13] [14]

During the battle at Blair, federal military officers were escorted to Logan County by local UMW leaders to assess the situation and to determine whether or not federal troops should be dispatched to the battlefield. A member of that group recalled, "The women seemed to say more than the men. They did not want the men to go back unless the United States troops were there to see that they were protected." Testifying under oath regarding the attitude of marchers in the field, that same team member (David Fowler) quoted a woman from Ramage (near Blair) who, when confronted with governor Morgan's order for the redneck army to disband, had exclaimed to him, "my God, Mr. Fowler, it would be all right if it were the union's affair, and we would say nothing; but it is not the union's affair and the people of West Virginia are here to protect their honor."[15]

That very same year at one of the hundreds of "teaching institutes" established by Conley's ACA throughout West Virginia, Mineral County teachers denounced the "Bolshevistic tendencies" of their fellow West Virginians who were coal laborers, recommending the "comprehensive teaching of Americanism, good citizenship, and morality to alleviate the problem."[16]

Through the ACA Conley successfully provided political cover for the coal owners association across the Kanawha field which, in an industry-wide sweep starting in 1922, began evicting from company housing as many as 50,000 union miners including their families, replacing them with strikebreakers.[17]

Over the short term Phil Conley's propaganda campaign effectively delayed the result intended by those who had marched to battle. The reign of terror by coal owners and the State of WV didn't effectively end until 1933, when it literally took an act of Congress to restore civil liberties back to miners and their families. Only 90 days after Roosevelt's National Industrial Recovery Act was passed, WV's southern coal fields were essentially unionized.[18]

> *West Virginia was very likely the first state in U.S. history to have been investigated by Congress for labor violations* **by the state's own government.** *Although the U.S. Senate committee revealed that State's governor and its lower courts had been violating the constitutional rights citizens as early as 1912 and recommend abolishing the mine guard system, the committee failed to re-establish justice due to its lack of jurisdiction.* Summary Report; Senate Committee on Education and Labor hearings pursuant to S. Res. 37, 63d Cong., March 9, 1914 (p. 4)

In 2010, respected WV historian and author David Alan Corbin spoke to a gathering hosted by the WV Humanities Council. Not far from the state capital in Charleston, Corbin spoke mainly of Matewan's heroic Police Chief Sid Hatfield and the galvanizing effect that his assassination had on the entire labor movement. Corbin also recalled the startling results of an informal survey that he'd taken decades earlier at a large central high school in the southern part of the state. Calling for a show of hands, he had begun that lecture asking "How many here know about America's largest armed rebellion since the Civil War?" Although the school auditorium had been packed with students and teachers from the entire school for his lecture, there was no response. Trying a second time, Corbin then added that thousands of armed miners had marched to battle right in that county.

Recalling that his clue had grabbed everyone's attention, Corbin confessed that he'd been shocked to find that no one in the room seemed even aware of the Battle of Blair Mountain, much less of its unique historic importance.[19]

Decades later in Charleston at the WV Arts and Humanities Council building, Corbin publicly criticized state education officials for purposely repressing what may well be the richest labor history of any state in the nation, "In 12 years in public schools in West Virginia, I, like others of my generation, never heard a thing about the great West Virginia Mine Wars." Corbin explained, "In high school, our textbook, 'West Virginia: Yesterday and Today,' discussed the importance of the coal industry to our state, but made no mention of coal miners. Nothing about the United Mine Workers."[20]

The State's active attempt to eliminate its own darkest actions from recorded history became obvious during the administration of WV governor Homer Adams Holt. While in office, he kept Roosevelt's badly needed New Deal Works Progress Administration money from flowing into the state until Roosevelt administrators agreed to purge the historic West Virginia Guide of an entire chapter on labor history. To this day Holt's strident efforts to erase the state's support of systemic corporate terrorism are excluded from his online bio as presented by the West Virginia Division of Archives and History. Nor can his revisionist efforts be found by searching the state's official online Electronic Encyclopedia. [21]

Homer Holt not only viewed the struggles of labor and all reports of the cruelty of corporate avarice as "subversive," he did everything within his power to keep it out of the texts of his day. Years earlier governor Hatfield, a Republican, had destroyed the printing presses of labor newspapers; then later governor Holt, a Democrat, established the State Publicity Commission to counter "negative publicity" from that era and to promote his interpretation of historic events for West Virginia.[22]

No matter how well-intentioned the authors of biased revisionism may have been, there can be dire results if generations of citizens are kept from understanding the whole truth.

At a recent press conference regarding the UMWA report on the explosion that killed 29 mine workers at Montcoal, West Virginia's Upper Big Branch (UBB) mine, Union president Cecil Roberts shattered the popular misconception that all deep mines were "accidents waiting to happen," a notion that had been wrongly promoted by the coal industry for years. Introducing the Union's incident report, which, in its very title tags the Upper Big Branch fatalities as "Industrial Homicide," Roberts made it clear that the term "accident" should never be misapplied to what caused that explosion. The UMWA Executive Summary reports the following:

> "The dangerous conditions that contributed to the explosion existed at the mine on a daily basis. These conditions, which represented gross violations of mandatory health and safety standards, were *not accidental*."[23] (Italics added for emphasis)

In contrast, the U.S. Department of Labor's Mine Safety and Health Administration (MSHA) used the term "accident" eighteen times within its 10 page Executive Summary alone, making it far more difficult to blame government officials for not shutting that mine down over the long-term pattern of obvious safety violations.[24]

The first report to be made public after the explosion was by a team of independent experts. Led by former MSHA head J. Davitt McAteer, it charged that the blast was, in no small part, *due to the inability of the state of West Virginia to protect the lives of miners.* Appropriately calling it "a political failure – a failure by the state's government to nurture and support strict safety standards for coal miners," the scathing 120 page study recommended (in part) that, "If miners' lives are to be safeguarded, the cozy relationship between high-ranking government officials and the coal industry must change, as must the relationship between the enforcement agency and the industry it regulates." While the UMWA's Executive Summary 'wholeheartedly agrees' with that assessment, both MSHA and the WV Office of Mining Safety Health and Training completely failed to address the issue.[25]

There is one point upon which all of the investigators of UBB universally agree: *If existing regulations had only been strictly enforced, the deadly explosion at Upper Big Branch could have been avoided.*

In his *Charleston Gazette* article "Reforms written in miners' blood," Paul J. Nyden wrote, "When people talk about the history of mine safety, there is 'before Farmington,' and there is 'after Farmington.'"

"Up until then, there was no rock dusting, no controlling the mine dust, which is basically gunpowder," said Gov. Joe Manchin, whose uncle John died in explosions that rocked Farmington No. 9 before dawn on Nov. 20, 1968."[26]

Even though Manchin lived in Farmington and was certainly old enough at the time of the incident to recall it, his recollection of the rock dusting details was completely inaccurate. Just after the blast, former Executive Vice President of Operations for Consolidated Coal Corp. admitted to reporters that "the workings [at Consol's Farmington mine] were heavily rock-dusted, which may account for the lack of fire and violence at the 'front' of the mine from which the 21 men escaped safely."[27]

Many years had passed since the Farmington disaster, yet Manchin quite explicitly recalled other details, almost as if he had been there, stating, "These were horrific explosions. The air was so bad. The fires were so hot." Manchin recalled. "There was no way mine rescuers, the bravest people I have ever been around, could go past certain points. Changes were much needed."[28]

It is important to note that the "certain points" to which Manchin referred were areas where had apparently chosen *not* to implement rock-dusting. Consol made that choice at Farmington before regulations required it. Massey's Upper Big Branch mine near Montcoal hadn't rock dusted *despite* regulations. *While Manchin was governor.*

In all fairness, the reason that Manchin could have been mistaken about rock dusting at Farmington was possibly because just after the incident, WV governor Hulett C. Smith had publicly stated "I would like to explain that this is an accident," pointedly adding, "I have confidence that the mining industry is seeing the most improved safety measures are being taken. We have experienced tragedy here many times before. Mining is a hazardous profession."[29]

Despite governor Smith's reassurances that West Virginia's coal operators had been doing all they possibly could to prevent "accidents" from "happening," other lawmakers nonetheless passed the long overdue Mining Safety and Health Act of 1969. Had state regulators simply enforced that law at Upper Big Branch, then the deadliest explosion in any WV coal operation since Farmington could have been avoided. Despite the McAteer panel's recommendation to do away with the "cozy relationship" between coal owners and their politicians, at this writing virtually nothing has changed politically to keep another such "accident" from "happening" again.[30]

Even historians and educators seeking to honestly portray the past frequently fall into the habit of using terms and contexts that distort the reality of events as they occurred. Today they speak and write of the Matewan Massacre which wasn't a massacre at all, but a shootout that took place when Police Chief Sid Hatfield attempted to force a group of coal owner's mercenaries to surrender their guns inside his jurisdiction. Witness accounts agree that both sides had weapons and both sides suffered casualties, yet the WV Dept. of Archives and History not only repeatedly refers to the incident as the "Matewan Massacre," on its website is featured an unidentified newspaper piece titled "*The Matewan Massacre*" which basically portrays the event as an ambush instead of a showdown. Taken by state-paid "historians" directly from the Logan Coal Association Collection and prominently placed online without being identified as propaganda, the article was very likely the original source of the term "massacre" to cleverly, but improperly, identified the incident.

To make matters worse, the WV Department of Education has long been encouraging West Virginia students to use the State Archives and History online *Time Trails* internet links and to visit the State's multimillion dollar "museum" at the Capitol Complex Cultural Center to study for "noted" historian Phil Conley's "Golden" accolade, unaware that they're being fed the lies of a hard core industrial propagandist.

West Virginia has long been recognized as one of the nation's areas most abundant in natural resources. By gilding her story over the last century, local politicians and their financiers have kept the state's natural born citizens among the poorest in the world. Phil Conley passed away years ago, but his legacy of sacrificing the truth for the sake of unfettered avarice still claims victims, buries evidence, and exonerates murderers.

Notes:
[1] Joe Gieger, *Golden Horseshoe* WV Archives and History Newsletter, p.1, vol.5, no.1 March 2004
[2] http://wvde.state.wv.us/goldenhorseshoe/about.html (WV Department of Education Golden Horseshoe webpage)
[3] Erica Green *Blair Mountain battle continues* NPR news broadcast (June 16, 2010)
[4] National Historic Landmark Theme Study on American Labor History pursuant to Public Law 102-101; (1991)
[5] Ibid.,

[6]Cecil Roberts testimony before the U.S. House Committee on Mining and Natural Resources, (February 21, 1991). Quoted in Green, *Taking History to Heart*, 147-165, which includes a fuller examination of sites of conflict in the South.

[7]Hennen, John C., *The Americanization of West Virginia*, Creating a Modern Industrial State 1916 -1925, p. 126 (1966) ,

[8] Blizzard, William C., *When Miners March*, p. 271; Oakland, CA: PM Press (2010_. Wess Harris, ed.

[9]Hennen, Ibid., p. 126

[10]Lunt, Richard D. Law and Order vs the Miners p. 158 – 159 Archon Books (1979)

[11]Geiger, Ibid.; WV Board of Education webpage:  http://wvde.state.wv.us/

[12]Kline, Michael *Appalachian Heritage* (Volume 59, No. 5, Summer 2011.)

[13]*Paternalism*; a Pocahantas Coal Operators' Association pamphlet: UMWA District 17 files UMWA archives, UMWA Headquarters, Washington, DC.

[14]Kelly, Jocelyn: *Rape in war,* U.S Institutes of Peace Special Report 243, (June 2010); Smith-Spark, Laura *How did rape become a weapon of war?* BBC News Special (Dec. 8, 2004)

[15]testimony: David Fowler, Red Jacket v John L. Lewis, 2: 2863

[16]Hennen, Ibid., p. 126

[17]*Lunt, Richard D. Law and Order Vs the Miners, West Virginia 1907–1933*; p. 166 Archon Books (1979)

[18]Ibid. p. 181

[19] Tom Rhule's personal notes and transcripts of an audio recording of Corbin's lecture.

[20]Nyden, Paul J. *Historian brings mine wars back to life* Charleston Gazette, May 23, 2010

[21]Thomas, Jerry B., *The Nearly Perfect State: Governor Homer Adams Holt, the WPA Writers' Project and the Making of West Virginia: A Guide to the Mountain State* WV ?? Volume 52 (1993), pp. 91-108)

[22]Ibid

[23]Executive Summary: *UMWA Industrial Homicide: Report on the Upper Big Branch Mine Disaster* p. 13

[24]Executive Summary*; U.S. Department of Labor's Mine Safety and Health Administration (MSHA) on Upper Big Branch Mine Disaste*r.

[25] WV Governor's Independent Investigation Panel Report on Upper Big Branch, May 19, 2011.

[26]Nyden, Paul J. *Reforms written in miners' blood*, Charleston Gazette, Nov. 23, 2008

[27] *78 miners entombed in no. 9 after blasts rip workings* Times-West Virginian, Nov. 21, 1968

[28] Nyden, Paul J. *Reforms written in miners' blood*, Charleston Gazette, Nov. 23, 2008

[29] Ibid Times-West Virginian

[30]McAteer quote from Charleston Gazette, Feb. 7, 2012 *Drug testing bill "a distraction,' McAteer says.*

*In 1991 three archeologists were hired by the WV Humanities Council to assess the historical value of Blair Mountain. They recommended that the State preserve the historic resource by permitting only the deep mining of coal at Blair, and to develop it into a monument with a battlefield museum and informational trails. Within a year WV's State Historic Preservation Officer granted permission to basically destroy the most prominent reminder of the State's dubious role in a war that was waged against it* by its own citizens.

# Handwritten Memories
## James Kilgore

In addition to being among our nation's most gifted folklorists and labor historians, Michael and Carrie Kline have produced numerous recordings of traditional music and have composed a large collection of original material.

James Kilgore was moved by the power of their song to share the following Handwritten Memories. —ed

1-09-10

Carrie + Michael Kline
114 Boundary Ave
Elkins WV 26241

Dear Folks:
I want to thank you so much For the great CD you sent me, I can hardly listen to it without tears in my eyes it brings back so many memories of my childhood, growing up in the old Clean Eagle coal camp where my daddy worked in the mines. I can still see the old coal tipple that ran day and night And C+O coal cars, passing Right behind our house.
Daddy played the guitar that sounded much like the music in your CD. Him and some of his miner FRiends would gather on the porch of the old Company Store and make some of the best music like yours. about every Sunday
My FAther in Law who worked the mines 44 yrs swears the Sixteen Ton song was made up on That Co. Store porch but we will never know.
My Dad went in the mines with his Dad when he was only 12 yrs old and died of silicosis when he was only 39 yrs old. Mother had passed away 7 yrs before From cancer she was only 29 yrs old leaving 4 children.

Pitston Coal Co made everyone move out of Clean Eagle in 1979 tore down all the houses but they can't tear down the memories, the good and the bad.

The coal miners in those days were a special breed, and the people in coal camps were like one big Family that really cared for each other its a shame to say it will never be the same again

The only thing that stayed the same is the Big Coal Cos. still use the miners For that Almighty dollar and nothing else matters to Them

My Dad died so young, my Father in law after working 44 yrs had to Fight the Co 7 yrs For his Black Lung by then he had Lost his Wife And was on a breathing machine. When you can't load another ton of coal you Are no use to the Company, its still that way today, He passed away in 92 Gasping For Another Breat

Here at the Logan Chief State park they have picking And singing in the park, people come From all over to pick And sing in Spring and Summer I would love to hear you play some music. I Am so glad Folks like you haven't Forgotten the old coal miners, so many people have Most have no idea what these men went through to make a living For their Families

These people running these big machines
taking off the mountain tops could not
carry the picks and shovels of the old
miners like my Dad, Grandpa and Father
in Law.
    When Massey is through they will
leave just the Coal Cos. have always
done.
    Thanks again For the CD I
will enjoy it very much.
                    Sincerly Yours
                    James D. Kilgore

Clean Eagle WV.

Clean Eagle West Virginia
Is A coal Camp Town I Know
Its Where my Daddy Worked The mine
So many Years Ago

I Remember to this very day
How the whites of his eyes would shine
I'd wonder how Black And dark it must be
To work down in that Mine
At Quitting Time us Kids would Run
To get Daddys dinner pail
He always left A Pie or Cake
He hardly ever would Fail

I remember well the Company Store
And to its door we'd Skip
To spend a Nickel dime or so
Or money they called Scrip

These thing are cherished memories
But Strange For now I Find
For here I work As Daddy did
In the Darkness of A mine
Clean Eagle still was where I lived
With my wife and Sons so Fine
For them I dream of better-Things
Than working in this Mine

Clean Eagle is Filled with memories
Some good and some so Bad
But As For me It comes to mind        James Kilgore
When I Remember mom & DAD              1979

Published In the Logan Banner when Pittston made
                                      Everyone move out.

# A Rare Breed

Once there was a Breed of men
None like them any more
A tough and Hardy Group of Souls
They worked the mines Long Before

They wore no Fancy Striped Clothes
With A modern shining Lamp
They spit into a Carbide Light
And Lived in An old Coal Camp

They did not Run a big Machine
Pick And Shovel were their Tools
And hauled their coal to Bright Sunlight
Behind some worn out Mules

The work was Hard The wages Small
Yet each day they made that trip
To crawl in darkness Long Long hours
And maybe draw some Scrip.

This Rare Breed Are passing By
Grandpa, Dad, or Old Friend
These real Black Diamond Miners
Won't come this Way Again

Some may Lay on A Hill of Green
Or under a mountain to not be seen
Dust Filled Lungs that never mend
Grandpa, Dad or Dear Old Friend

Most Are gone, their Journey Through
This Breed of men Are now so Few
The Flames Are out on Carbide Lamps
Only memories Left of Old Coal Camps

James D. Kilgore

Within the following pamphlet readers are offered an unadulterated perspective from the operator's union.

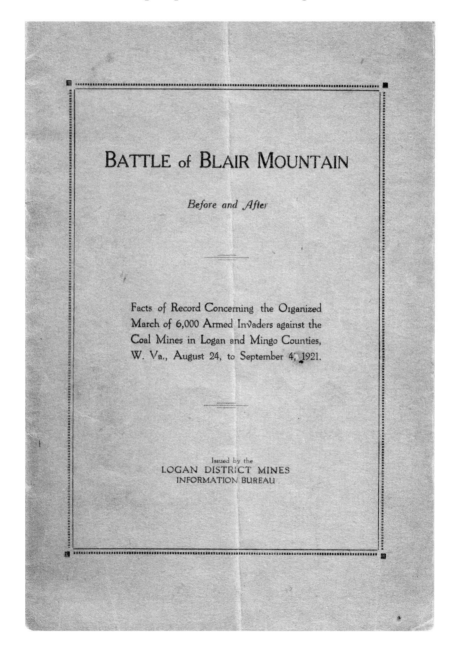

BATTLE of BLAIR MOUNTAIN

*Before and After*

Facts of Record Concerning the Organized
March of 6,000 Armed Invaders against the
Coal Mines in Logan and Mingo Counties,
W. Va., August 24, to September 4, 1921.

Issued by the
LOGAN DISTRICT MINES
INFORMATION BUREAU

Statement of
## GOVERNOR E. F. MORGAN,
of West Virginia

---

"I have not participated and am not interested in the program of the United Mine Workers of America in extending their organization into the non-union coal fields of West Virginia.

"I have not participated and am not interested in the efforts of the coal operators in the non--union fields in opposing unionization.

"I AM INTERESTED, however, both as an official and a citizen in the maintenance of law and the preservation of order, and all the force at my command will be used to require those engaged in labor strife, whether operator or miner, union or non-union, to obey the laws of the State."

# BATTLE of BLAIR MOUNTAIN

THROUGHOUT the seventeen years during which commercial coal has been mined in the Logan district of West Virginia, strikes, shut-downs or other labor troubles have been practically unknown in this flourishing field.

Similarly, industrial peace reigned in Mingo county, adjoining Logan on the southwest, until the spring of 1920 when refusal of the coal producers to negotiate contracts with the United Mine Workers of America was followed by repeated acts of lawlessness. Martial law was then proclaimed throughout the district, and thereafter has remained in force.

As soon as martial law was proclaimed, the United Mine Workers established tent colonies for its members in the district. The last census as of July 18, 1821, records a tent colony population of 1304 men, women and children living in idleness while enjoying weekly payments from the treasury of the United Mine Workers.

Adjoining Logan county on the northeast is Boone county, where the mine workers are organized. Kanawha county, in which mobilization for the armed invasion of Aug. 24---Sept. 4 took place, adjoins Boone county, and also is organized.

It will thus be seen that Logan county was the "Belgium" of the attempted invasion. On the crest of a mountain range dividing Logan and Boone, defenders took their positions to check the oncoming rush of the invaders. An Associated Press dispatch dated Washington, Sept. 17, refers to the invasion as follows:

> "It was in protest against the enforcement of martial lay and to compel unionization of the Mingo county mines that the miners' army started its march, stopping only when Federal troops intervened."

The Logan mine owners and their employes started operations on Thanksgiving Day, 1904, working under a non-union agreement. This agreement—never disputed by employes or producers—has continued in uninterrupted force. Industrial harmony has blessed the region. Now, as in past years, union miners are given employment without prejudice, the only stipulation being that they refrain from exploiting their union affiliation while working in the Logan field. Approximately 50 per cent of Logan workers on today's payrolls are men who formerly held active membership in the United Mine Workers of America.

The Logan district mines produce about 35 per cent of West Virginia's total output of coal, from non-union mines. Approximately one-tenth of all the bituminous coal mined in the world comes from West Virginia fields. Domination of the present non-union fields by the United Mine Workers of America would place that organization in industrial command of the bituminous situation.

Governor Morgan describes the recent attempted invasion as "an organized outbreak against the law and constituted authorities in the southern section of this State (West Virginia)". Newspapers throughout the country called it the "March Against Logan and Mingo," and referred to the several days' bitter fighting as the "Battle of Blair Mountain."

A score or more of men were killed. Many were wounded. The invaders took possession of trains carrying United States mails; forced unwilling men and boys to join their ranks; looted stores; and ignored President Harding's proclamation calling upon them to disperse and disarm. United States army troops were sent to the scene in response to Governor Morgan's appeal for Federal aid. The cost of transporting and maintaining these troops is placed at more than $1,000,000. Loss in wages to the Kanawha district miners, and loss to the Kanawha district producers because of the virtual closing down of all work, totaled an estimated loss of more than $500,000 up to September 4.

Both the Logan and Kanawha districts are served by the Chesapeake & Ohio Railroad. The official loading reports of the C. & O. recorded during the period of the attempted invasion, supplies proof of how the earnings of the miners in the Logan and Kanawha districts were effected. Under normal conditions, production in the respective fields is substantially the same—about 750 cars per day each.

The miners are paid on the amount of tonnage produced. The C. & O. reports are based on 50-ton car shipments. Following are the daily shipments from Aug. 19 to Sept. 9, inclusive—supplying proof of the extent to which men from the organized field in Kanawha district participated in the invasion:

| Date | Logan Dist. Cars | Kanawha Dist. Cars |
|---|---|---|
| Aug. 19 | 661 | 410 |
| "   22 | 626 | 211 |
| "   23 | 552 | 299 |
| "   24 | 610 | 214 |
| "   25 | 541 | 184 |
| "   26 | 791 | 152 |
| "   27 | 423 | 38 |
| "   29 | 697 | 25 |
| "   30 | 462 | 133 |
| "   31 | 453 | 180 |
| Sept. 1 | 451 | 122 |
| "    2 | 511 | 125 |
| "    3 | 458 | 67 |
| "    5 | 725 | 61 |
| "    7 | 637 | 267 |
| "    8 | 712 | 405 |
| "    9 | 696 | 492 |
| Total....10,006 cars | 3,385 cars |
| 500,300 tons | 169,250 tons |

The above table shows that during the height of the trouble the Logan miners were paid for producing 331,050 more tons of coal than the Kanawha miners, enabling the distribution of more than three times the amount of wages in the Logan district as compared with the Kanawha field.

The 6,000 or more men who took part in the armed invasion mobilized in Kanawha and Boone counties, and recruits came from Fayette and Raleigh counties which comprise the New River District. The mine owners in these fields operate under contract with the United Mine Workers of America. District 17, U. M. W. of A., with headquarters in Charleston, capital of West Virginia, has jurisdiction over the State.  C. F. Keeney is president, and Fred Mooney, secretary, of District 17.

At the time of the invasion there was no controversy of any nature whatsoever between the Kanawha, Boone, Raleigh and Fayette county producers and their employes.  No strike existed—none was impending.

The Kanawha Coal Operators Association, having as members the mine owners of these counties, acts in matters of mutual interest between employes and employers.

Early in August, Association members reported that their employes were not living up to the contracts entered into with the United Mine Workers of America. The miners had submitted no grievances.  The subject of wage reductions had not been raised.  In view of conditions which the union producers said were becoming alarming, the following letter was prepared and forwarded:

"Mr. C. F. Keeney, Pres.,
District 17, U. M. W. of A.,
Charleston, W. Va.
Dear Sir.—

I am writing you to protest against the serious situation existing in the Kanawha district, occasioned by members of your organization.

For the last two weeks men have been traveling over this district meeting with members of the committees at the various coal mines, agitating men to congregate, in certain parts of this district, which has been done.  Complaints are coming into this office from practically all over the district that mines have been closed in violation of contract.

It is unnecessary for me to state to you the situation existing in this district, and the high cost of producing coal resulting.  These unwarranted shut-downs only aggravate the tense situation and further increase the cost of production.

We have refrained, so far, from asking you to amend our contract looking toward a reduction in wages, and we must insist upon your organization doing everything in your power to insist upon your membership complying with the contract that exists between the operators and miners of this district.

I trust it will be your pleasure to immediately get in touch with the situation and correct the abuses complained of.

Very truly yours,

(Signed) D. C. KENNEDY,
Sec'y-Comm'r Kanawha Coal Operators Association."

Keeney made no reply to this letter, a copy of which was sent to John Lewis, international president of the United Mine Workers of America. Lewis replied as follows:

"Indianapolis, Ind.,
August 24, 1921.

Mr. D. C. Kennedy, Sec'y-Comm'r
Kanawha Coal Operators Association,
Kanawha Valley Bank Building,
Charleston, W. Va.

Dear Sir :—

I am in receipt of your letter of Aug. 22, transmitting copy of communication which you have addresssed to President Keeney of District 17 on the same date. I advise that the subject matter will be given every consideration by this office.

Yours very truly,
(Signed) JOHN L. LEWIS, President,
United Mine Workers of America."

Except for the above letter, no further communication was received from Lewis.

Briefly stated the reasons for the attempted invasion of Mingo county through Logan county, are as follows:

When in July, 1920, the Mingo mines decided to continue a non-union agreement with their men, the United Mine Workers called a strike. Lawlessness ensued. The Tug river, separating Mingo county from Kentucky, is about fifty feet from bank to bank. Rifle and pistol

PROSPEROUS MINERS BUILT    UP THIS BUSINESS CENTRE

SEVENTEEN years of uninterrupted thrift and contentment have established Logan, West Virginia, in a unique and enviable position among the coal centres of this country. Freedom from strikes, shutdowns and other labor disturbances that have afflicted neighboring districts, has enabled Logan wage-earners to enjoy high standards of living. Their demands for high-grade clothing, food and home comforts have attracted wide-awake merchants to Logan. Modern stores (as you see in the above photo) occupy the sites along Logan's crowded business streets.

HOME-MAKERS in this flourishing community attribute their prosperity to working conditions under the American or open-shop plan. The miners have subscribed to this plan year after year, although about 50 per cent of their total number formerly were active members of union organizations. More than a quarter of the total deposits in Logan banks represent miners' savings. Among other things, seventy-two miles of railroad extensions have been built out of Logan since the first coal was shipped from there in 1904.

firing was directed from the Kentucky side of the Tug, thus involving Kentucky authority. By joint request of the Governors of Kentucky and West Virginia, martial law was declared in Mingo county. Since the issuance of the proclamation, crime in Mingo county has decreased more than 90 per cent.

"It was the enforcement of martial law in Mingo county," Governor Morgan says, "that was cited as a reason for the mobilization of the armed miners of Kanawha and Boone counties, who were later joined by armed bands from some of the mines in Raleigh and Fayette Counties.

"IT WAS ANNOUNCED THAT THE OBJECTIVE OF THE MARCH WAS TO RESIST MARTIAL LAW IN MINGO COUNTY.

"The insurrectionists exhibited their antipathy toward lay enforcement officers on August 12, near Sharples, Boone county, when an armed body of sixty men held-up, disarmed and robbed two State policemen, and ordered them to leave Boone county. On the night of August 19, at Edwight, an attempt was made to assassinate another State policeman.

He was shot in the back by an armed body of men which left Edwight the following morning for Lens creek. These armed bodies continued to assemble on Lens Creek (about ten miles from Charleston), patrolling the roads, halting and using railroad trains, pillaging stores of arms, ammunition and supplies, and invading private homes in search of guns."

During the week beginning August 14, agitators visited the mining camps in the Kanawha and adjacent districts and in public speeches told the United Mine Workers to prepare for the invasion of Logan and Mingo. Between 200 and 300 men had assembled at Marmet, on Lens creek on August 20. From this number, delegates were sent back to each mine in the Kanawha field bearing tidings that the armed march was about to start. "Orders" were given to United Mine Workers to arm and report at Marmet. Guards were posted along the roads leading to Marmet.

On the night of Wednesday, August 24, between 3000 and 4000 armed men were assembled. The advance started. Governor Morgan describes the situation at this stage as follows:

> "The officers of Kanawha county advised me they were unable to cope with the situation or disperse the insurgents, and on the following day I requested Federal troops. I felt that Federal troops were necessary because the National Guard (disbanded following the world war) had not yet been reorganized under a law that had been effective for less than thirty days, and the State police were engaged in the enforcement of martial law in Mingo county and distributed at their stations in various parts of the State. (The total roster of State Police at this time was about 100 men).

"MY OPTION WAS TO ASK FOR FEDERAL TROOPS OR ASK FOR CITIZEN VOLUNTEERS TO REPEL THE INVASION. TO SAVE BLOODSHED, I CHOSE TO ASK THE FEDERAL GOVERNMENT FOR TROOPS."

Instead of sending troops, Secretary of War Weeks ordered Brigadier-General H. H. Bandholtz to the scene. On his arrival, Gen Bandholtz conferred with Keeney and Mooney and other officers of the United Mine Workers, demanding that they proceed forthwith to Madison where the armed march had halted after advancing about forty-five miles from Charleston. The demand was obeyed. The march was stopped. All except about 1,200 of the 6,000 armed men who composed the "army" at this time, scattered in the mountains. They took with them machine guns, high-power rifles, thousands of rounds of ammunition, and provisions.

The following night, August 27, Captain J. R. Brockus, of the State Police and a squad of men crossed the Logan line from Mingo into Boone county, near Sharples, to serve warrants on forty men wanted by Sheriff Don Chafin, of Logan county. Proceeding down Beech creek, Brockus encountered armed men patrolling the roads. Two patrols surrendered. A third answered Brockus' commands with a volley of bullets. The fire was returned. Three men were killed during the encounter.

News of the fight was carried by the miners' couriers to the men who had turned back from the invasion, supposedly for their homes.

Within twenty-four hours, more than 6,000 armed men had assembled with headquarters at Jeffrey. Under army-like formation, they advanced toward the rugged mountains separating Blair from Logan.

Meantime, word of the renewed invasion had sped through the southwest territory of the state. Volunteers from many sections started for Logan on the double-quick to aid in resisting the advance. An example of the personnel of this volunteer force is contained in the following resolution later passed by McDowell county authorities:

> "The citizens of this county, miners, American Legion members, doctors, lawyers, merchants, bankers, laborers, clerks and others, 1229 in number, upon the call of the Governor, nobly responded as volunteers in defense of the laws of the country."

In the van of volunteers from the Pocahontas field were three score American Legion members. Charleston business and professional men added their quotas.

The volunteer army of defense took up positions along a 15-mile line on the mountain crests about two miles west of Blair. Attack followed attack by the invaders. "No Man's Land" was swept by machine gun bullets and the fire of sharpshooters. The fighting continued almost unceasingly for four days. On September 2, Federal troops arrived in the State, some of them taking up positions in Logan, others proceeding to Madison, Sharples, Jeffrey, Clothier and Blair. As the troops advanced, detachments of the miners surrendered and dispersed. But even while the troops occupied the area, some of the heaviest fighting of the invasion was taking place at the front. The troops were forced to penetrate to advanced positions before the dispersal became general. A majority of the miners did not bring their arms with them when they surrendered.

At no time did the defenders seek to advance. Efforts were centered on keeping the insurrectionists from invading Logan.

Much has been said about the so-called "mine guards" in the Logan field. Logan county comprises 400 square miles with a population of 60,000. Law enforcement over this far-flung area is maintained by eight constables, and as many State Police as occasion requires. Of the later, half a dozen were on duty at the time of the attempted invasion. When fighting started, however, less than a hundred others were rushed to the scene. Prior to August 24, twenty-four deputy sheriffs were on duty in Logan. Through an arrangement with the County Court of Logan, the mining companies were paying the salaries of 19 deputies although these deputies serving under the Sheriff of Logan county, collected taxes and performed similar duties. They neither came into contact with, nor had authority over the miners in the day's work.

They received a small extra compensation for the extra work of guarding the mines' semi-monthly payroll. This payroll called for the disbursal of about $500,000 in cash every two weeks. Because of insurance requirements, the deputies guarded this cash in the absence of other law-enforcement officers.

Prior to the acceptance of a deputy, the Circuit Judge passes on the candidate's character and demands a bond for the privilege of carrying arms. The financial burden of deputy-sheriff employment will be spared mine owners as soon as the State carries out its law enforcement pro-gramme now nearing completion. Until then—as during past years—the protection of life and property must be undertaken by the mine owners in the only way provided by law.

At the time of the attempted invasion, Keeney and Mooney were fugitives from justice, indictments having been returned against them in Williamson, Mingo county, on charges of murder in connection with a shooting affray in Mingo county last May.

On Sept. 17, Keeney, Mooney and W. H. Blizzard, who is alleged to have led the attempted invasion, were among 500 men indicted at Logan on charges of murder, insurrection or carrying weapons. Of this number, about 400 are charged specifically with murder.

The murder indictments returned were based on the Red Man Act. Section 10 of the Act reads:

> "If two or more persons under the name of 'Red Men', 'regulators', 'Vigilance Committee', or any other name or without a name, combine or conspire together for the purpose of destroying, injuring, or taking and carrying away any property, real or personal, not their own, every such person whether he has done any act in pursuance of such combination or conspiracy or not, shall be guilty of a misde-

meanor and fined not less than fifty, nor more than five
hundred dollars, and may, at the discretion of the court,
be confined in jail not less than one or more than twelve
months."

Section 13 reads:

"If the death of any person shall result from the commission of any offense mentioned in the tenth section of this
chapter, every person engaged in the commission of such
offense shall be guilty of murder of the first degree, and
punished as in other cases of murder of the first degree."

Keeney and Mooney surrendered in Charleston on
Sept. 18 and were taken to the Williamson jail.   John L.
Lewis immediately communicated with Governor Morgan
as follows:

"In view of the fact that President C. F. Keeney and Secretary-
Treasurer Fred Mooney, of District 17, United Mine Workers of
America, have surrendered to the authorities of West Virginia in
answer to grand jury indictments previously rendered against them,
I sincerely hope that your office will take every necessary step to
insure the safety of their persons and lives.  This request is necessi-
tated by the fact that formerly members of the United Mine Workers
of West Virginia who became prisoners of the commonwealth were
subjected to personal indignities resulting in certain instances in
loss of life.  The mine workers of the country sincerely hope that
the authority of your office will be ample to protect Messrs. Keeney
and Mooney from circumstances of this character.  I also express
the hope that similar treatment will be accorded all members of the
United Mine Workers of America now imprisoned or under indictment in West Virginia."

Replying to the above communication, Governor Morgan said:

"Your appeal to the constituted authorities of this State follows within a few hours of your public statement that the State
government of West Virginia had broken down.  Your belated recognition that our government is functioning is complete refutation
of your previous statement.  Keeney and Mooney, of course, will
have the protection of the authorities.  However,
IF YOU HAD SHOWN THE SAME SOLICITATION FOR THE
POOR TOILING MEMBERS OF YOUR ORGANIZATION WHO
WERE INCITED AND COERCED INTO INSURRECTION
that you now display for its officers, Keeney and Mooney, many lives
would have been saved, hundreds of members of your organization
would not be standing under indictments, and the good name of West
Virginia would not have been maligned from one end of this country
to the other."

*"A history museum is as good as the history that goes into it, and the West Virginia State Museum is based on the very best scholarship available to this generation. Top historians were involved from start to finish and their thoughtful work underlies every part of our spectacular new museum"*
—Ken Sullivan, West Virginia Humanities Council.

## STATE MUSEUM HISTORIANS

Dr. Ron Eller            Dr. Jerry Thomas
Dr. Ron Lewis            Dr. John Williams
Dr. Ken Sullivan

"The historians were not paid for their work, so it didn't make a lot of sense to keep revising the text and asking them to review the material a second time (for free)."

—Stan Bumgardner,
Creative Director for the West Virginia State Museum,
March 9, 2010

74

# Victory on Blair Mountain!
Wess Harris

Originally published in *Appalachian Heritage* (Volume 59, No. 5, Summer 2011.)

Who really won the Battle of Blair Mountain? In retrospect it certainly wasn't the combined forces of the coal association and the state of West Virginia, as it has been wrongfully portrayed by the state's own historians and in the media. Considering the full context of the record as we know it today, all of the main goals for which the miners marched were accomplished. Though it took several years after the battle for the mine workers and their families to see the changes, few historians have ever recognized that this particular violent struggle in rural Appalachia was for far higher stakes than their "official" historical accounts ever originally claimed.

The first Battle of Blair Mountain, fought in 1921, was the largest armed insurrection since the Civil War. Logan County, West Virginia saw a battle between ten thousand Union miners and their supporters determined to take the U.S. Constitution to southern West Virginia and perhaps half that many well armed mercenaries fighting for the corporate interests seeking to keep unionization from the coal fields. The original battle was sparked by the murder of Matewan's pro-Union Chief of Police, Sid Hatfield, by Baldwin-Felts gun thugs in the employ of local coal operators. The real cause of the conflict ran much deeper.

Market pressures pitted labor costs in the heavily unionized northern coal fields against the nonunion southern fields. Perhaps most importantly, life in nonunion camps had become intolerable. This went far beyond merely wanting the Union. No longer would miners endure being told they could not visit with neighbors. No longer would miners suffer evictions, beatings, and even death for daring to speak their minds. No longer could miners tolerate coal companies forcing their women into sexual servitude to keep their children from starving. It had become personal. There were scores to settle. The Union provided hope that the freedom and dignity won for the Europeans in the Great War and the promise of the United States Constitution could now become reality for the miners of southern West Virginia.

Today, the battle continues as coal companies want to mine the mountain using mountain removal technology that will destroy the mountain and, they hope, any memory of the earlier battle. The prevailing narrative that the battle of Blair Mountain was a defeat for the miners is generally accepted by scholars, government agencies, coal companies, and even Union supporters looking back with pride on a noble but unsuccessful effort. Well-intentioned scholars, facing a wall of silence from miners maintaining a tradition of secrecy and a less than accurate spin from a variety of seemingly authoritative sources, have long repeated a tale of defeat that no longer withstands scrutiny. However pervasive and time tested, this spin on events fails to meet the major requirement of any historical interpretation: external validity. The time has come to re-evaluate standard interpretations of Blair Mountain and its significance.

Viewing the events on Blair Mountain as a "crushing defeat" for the miners (Meador, p.63) is an understandable if fatally flawed interpretation resulting in no small part from a compartmentalization of our understanding of events: Mine Wars – Paint Creek, Cabin Creek, Blair Mountain – were fought and miners were defeated. Historian David Corbin observes that in the early 1930s, "Overnight, mine workers flocked to the union." (p. 161) This seemingly spontaneous organization appears as a unique event untied to the earlier "defeats." Providing a view of history that is internally consistent, externally valid, and of use to modern youth as they build a future, mandates a major change of paradigm. From defeat to victory; from isolated mine wars to a fully connected thread, the Great West Virginia Mine War: 1890 to the present. Blair Mountain was not a distinct "mine war" that the Union lost, it was a battle the Union won.

Militarily, current knowledge leads to the inescapable conclusion that the Red Neck Army, Union miners wearing red bandanas as a uniform, was on the brink of victory with operators desperately calling for federal intervention. Archaeologist Brandon Nida offers the following take on the oft imagined Union defeat:

"In our initial analysis, the archaeological evidence indicates that the miners were much more successful in their assault. Multiple sites have been discovered that show intense close quarter combat, with incoming bullet slugs and short range ammunition casings. All the evidence points to a different narrative than is usually told. Instead of the coal operator forces being able to hold off the miners but yet for some reason frantically calling for federal troops, the coal operators were instead frantically calling in the federal troops because their positions were being overrun by the miners."

Readers may wonder how it happened that 10,000 Union miners each possessed a red bandana to wear as identification in battle. Did not some prefer blue or white or yellow? While early miners were treated as contractors required to pay for their own tools and supplies, the ever generous coal companies provided red —and only red— bandanas free of charge.

—All the better to mask the color of blood when, not if, injuries occurred!

Without question the intervention of federal troops brought about the end of fighting on Blair Mountain. In retrospect, the troops certainly did not come to further the Union cause. Yet not a shot was fired between the federal troops and the Red Neck Army. Bill Blizzard, leader of Union forces, actually approached the arriving troops. Miners, many veterans of the Great War and others, survivors of digging the coal that fed the American Navy, welcomed the arrival of "Our Boys." While one need not look far to find accounts describing the troops as suppressing the revolt or defeated miners surrendering, the reality at the time was likely quite different. Archeologist Harvard Ayers, long time Blair Mountain researcher, is clear: "Absent the feds, I believe that the miners may have overrun the coal operators, and it would have been a bloody mess." When troops arrived, miners did not envision defeat. Far from surrendering, miners welcomed the troops as would any weary front line fighter being offered a chance to withdraw from the front and be replaced by fresh troops. Our Boys had arrived. Robert Shogan reminds us that as the miners marched from Blair Mountain, "many of them waved American flags." (p. 223) It is noteworthy that Blizzard, known but unnamed leader of the miners, was not arrested as would be any leader of a rebellion. He was free to go and allowed to keep his weapon. Hardly how a defeated rebel is treated!

Following the Battle and the disbursement of the Red Neck Army, hundreds of indictments were handed out to those who fought. Unable to defeat the Union on the field of battle, coal operators found it necessary to seek destruction of the Union using the courts. Not a single federal indictment was forthcoming but the Great State of West Virginia sought to hang Union leaders on charges ranging from arson to treason –against the state! A series of trials for Blizzard and others resulted in Union victory as they had been destined to win on the Mountain. While some minor convictions occurred, the trials resulted in acquittals for Blizzard and other key figures. Not a single Union miner was hanged. Blizzard's execution could well have led to a similar fate for the leadership of other major American unions. A mere five years after the Russian revolution, the leadership of the entire American labor movement was at risk. American capitalists were in no mood to coddle uppity workers. A change of venue resulted in the 1922 trials being held in the Eastern

Panhandle town of Charles Town, West Virginia. Big Coal could not manage to rid themselves of Blizzard despite providing its own attorneys as prosecutors. (Blizzard, p. 322-3) When a verdict of acquittal came in, the citizens of Charles Town opened the American Legion Hall to make available fife and drum for a parade of celebration. Labor leaders around the country breathed a bit easier –and longer.

The prevailing "defeated" narrative views the decline of the Union in West Virginia throughout the 1920s as a result of the cost of the battle and the trials that followed. A depleted treasury could not support the cost of organizing. Seldom does West Virginia lead the nation, but throughout the '20s we were at the forefront of the Depression. Demand for coal and coal miners was low. Organizing against Big Coal was not likely to be successful no matter the resources available. Further, organizing in West Virginia throughout the '20s was hardly a priority for the Union. Rather than attempt to exploit the strong military showing on Blair Mountain and subsequent victories in the courts, International President John L. Lewis sought to consolidate his organizational control. David Corbin, writing in *The West Virginia Encyclopedia*, declares that Lewis "withdrew the autonomy of District 17, precipitating a collapse of the UMWA in southern West Virginia" (p. 480). To the extent that this collapse was a defeat, it was precipitated by the action of the International leadership of the Union, not by any actions of the miners on Blair Mountain or at the subsequent trials.

Only in 1932 did the Union re-emerge as a major force in West Virginia. The nature of the resurgence sheds light on the meaning of the victory of Blair Mountain. Blizzard left the Union payroll shortly after the trials. International President John L. Lewis was not a fan of a grassroots leader who could prove tough to control and might become a rival. Yet throughout the 1920s Blizzard represented the Union as an unpaid lobbyist at the West Virginia state legislature. Indeed, from 1922 until 1955 he served the Union each session. In 1932 when FDR made unionization possible, Lewis recalled Blizzard to paid service for the Union. The military and legal victories of Blair Mountain began to show results.

Blair Mountain gave the people of the coal fields a hero in the person of Bill Blizzard. While some claimed that the absent District 17 officers Fred Mooney and Frank Keeney "managed events behind the scenes" (Keeney, WV Encyclopedia, p. 66) and others that Blizzard "did not command the army; he did not make its decisions or issue its orders. His acquittal in his later trial for treason demonstrated that" (Savage, p. 120). The miners knew better. They knew Mooney and Keeney lacked email and wireless. Mooney makes it quite clear, "We kept in touch with developments through the press reports and by messenger until September 16" (p. 99). The miners kept a code of silence that shaded the events of Blair Mountain for decades. The victory of Blair Mountain is best understood as having three components: The Union was winning militarily, won in the court room, and most importantly, emerged with a leadership cadre that would go on to organize West Virginia in the early '30s and lead the miners of West Virginia until beyond mid-century.

John L. Lewis understood and hoped to harness and control the leadership treasure that came from Blair Mountain. We know in retrospect that Lewis was a classic autocrat in terms of leadership style. Blizzard, by contrast, emerged and remained very much of the grassroots. The two were oil and water yet both spent their lives growing the same organization. In the early '30s, Lewis placed Blizzard back in District 17 to organize and organize he did. But Lewis insured that Bill was on a short leash. Famed District 17 was Provisional District 17 –provided John L. wanted it to be a district! (WCB, interviews, 2004-8) Bill was to serve under Van Bittner whom Lewis imported from Pennsylvania to run the district and get credit for any organizing that occurred. If Blizzard did the organizing, Lewis controlled the credits. The last entry of Corbin's mine war anthology is of the August 1, 1933, UMWJ article reporting on the June 23 convention in Charleston at which 2500 miners attended. The article mentions Bittner no fewer than six (6!) times and Blizzard not once, yet it was Blizzard who made the convention happen (WCB). Lewis made certain that Blizzard would always be a supporting cast member. C.B. Keeney labels Blizzard a "protégé" or "close associate" of Bittner yet nothing could be further from the truth. (various editions, WV Encyclopedia). Blizzard worked under Bittner in the organizational structure but the hero of Blair Mountain was hardly a protégé of a chap from Pennsylvania who was absent from Blair Mountain, rode around in a Cadillac (preferably with a driver), kept a mistress on the top floor of a Charleston hotel, and expected the staff to call him "Boss." Blizzard drove himself around in a Chevy. Despite repeated attempts, this author could never get William C. Blizzard to agree that his father would so much as join Bittner for a social cup of coffee. Readers may judge which of the two were more likely to find a following among the coal diggers of West Virginia!

The years that follow Blair Mountain are far more meaningfully understood when we view the events of 1921-22 as victories rather than defeats. The cadre of leaders that emerged from the Battle—Blizzard and his lifelong friends Charley Payne, Ed Holstein, and others— would lead the Union in West Virginia for decades. Blizzard's grassroots popularity gave Lewis the membership numbers he needed to get those sweet contracts: pensions, health care, safety provisions and the like. Blizzard got his status not because the Red Neck Army was defeated but because they were victors. It just took a few years to *look* like a win!

The great threat of the Red Neck Army and their strong showing on Blair Mountain, even as the International tried to stop the march, is the power of grassroots organizing. Power comes from either money or people and Blair Mountain was one Battle that the people won. The operators, the government, and sadly, even our Union, for years tried to distort the meaning of events that occurred. Historians of all political leanings have all too often been complicit in repeating tales of defeat. Looking back, Blair Mountain was a victory by people no longer willing to be controlled, exploited, and violently abused from above. The Union miners of West Virginia were tired of losing; we were learning how to win.

# Notes:

Ayers, Harvard *Unpublished Correspondence* (Appalachian Community Services, Inc. archives, 4/27/2011.)

Blizzard, William C. *Unpublished interviews with Wess Harris* (2004-2008.)

Blizzard, William C. *When Miners March* (PM Press, Oakland, CA 2010.)

Corbin, David Alan *The West Virginia Mine Wars – An Anthology* (Appalachian Editions, Martinsburg, WV, 1997.)

Keeney, C.B. *Bill Blizzard/ The West Virginia Encyclopedia* (WV Humanities Council, Charleston, WV, 2006)

Meador, Michael M. *The Red Neck War of 1921/ Goldenseal Book of the West Virginia Mine Wars* (Pictorial Histories, Charleston, WV, 1991.)

Mooney, Fred *Struggle in the Coal Fields* (West Virginia University Library, Morgantown, WV, 1967.)

Nida, Brandon *unpublished correspondence* (Appalachian Community Services, Inc. archives, 8/17/2011.)

Savage, Lon *Thunder in the Mountains* (Jalamap Publications, South Charleston, WV, 1984.)

Shogan, Robert *Battle of Blair Mountain* (Westview Press, Boulder, CO, 2004.)

# Baseball and Treason
## By Bill Kovarik

Bill Kovarik is a Professor of Communication at Radford University. This article appeared originally in *APPALACHIAN VOICE*.

Nothing can match it in the history of baseball. Check the visiting players' lineup:

Bill Blizzard, Right field. Charges: *Treason, murder*.

Cecil Sullivan, First base. Charge: *Murder*

Bill Blizzard (with bat) pauses between court sessions for a publicity photo with his team. During the Battle of Blair Mountain and his trial Blizzard was portrayed by the coal owners and their local media as the "Generalissimo" who led a bloodthirsty army of bomb-throwing Bolsheviks.

Okey Burgess, Second base. Charge: *Murder*

W. Lacey,   Third base. Charge: *Treason*

The fans around the fields of Charles Town, WV, knew that these were not minor leaguers. The stakes couldn't have been higher in the game that brought town residents and indicted union organizers together that spring of 1922.

The organizers were on trial for their roles in the Battle of Blair Mountain. A conviction on murder and treason charges would mean execution. The charges stemmed from an uprising against the coal industry following its assassination of a county sheriff sympathetic to miners.

Around 30 men had been killed in the uprising when the coal companies fought over 10,000 miners at the Battle of Blair Mountain in the spring of 1921. Now 200 miners were in Charles Town for trial. No one from the coal companies had faced similar indictments.

The coal companies demanded the death penalty for their opponents and the State of West Virginia had been more than obliging, allowing coal company lawyers to prosecute the cases on its behalf. Even the indictments had been written in the law offices of the coal companies.

The companies assumed they could convince a Jefferson County jury that the union men were desperate traitors. At a time of national hysteria about the Bolshevik threat, a treason and murder trial against admitted insurrectionists must have seemed like an easy dinger—and maybe even a grand slam. They would legally execute dozens, jail thousands, and crush organized labor once and for all.

But the companies had made a serious mistake. Between court sessions, they were entertaining themselves at a swank, out-of-town hotel. The accused union members, meanwhile, were playing baseball with the citizens of the town—the very people whose friends and neighbors were sitting on the jury. History hinges on moments like these common interests.

The trial had begun with a change of venue from Logan County, where the Battle of Blair Mountain was fought, to Jefferson County, near Harpers Ferry, West Virginia. Once the location was set, union organizers approached the businessmen's associations, hotels and private citizens for help sheltering the 200 miners and their families headed for Charles Town. When they arrived at the train station, wearing pink lapel ribbons identifying them as UMWA defendants, a cheering crowd marched them to the fire station's public hall.

In the lead role, Bill Blizzard, a handsome young man with a lovely spouse and two children along for the trial, maintained a cheerful attitude, as if he were not facing the gallows.

Blizzard's son and biographer, William C. Blizzard, wrote in the recently published book *When Miners March*: "The miners were out to make friends and they passed up few opportunities," and "The citizens of Charles Town learned that these supposed revolutionists were, after all, not very different from themselves."

They organized a baseball team and they made a point of attending church with their families in the town.

The miners were good at baseball, Blizzard wrote, but they were careful not to win too many games against the Charles Town citizens. When they did win, the proceeds from the game were donated to a hospital fund.

The first trial brought two dozen of the UMWA organizers into court, and Blizzard was named as the lead defendant. His union attorneys faced prejudice from the first, as the coal companies were allowed to keep secret their evidence and witness list. Blizzard's attorneys also protested the fact that groups of well armed coal company gunmen were present in the courtroom.

The first prosecution witness, state governor Ephriam Morgan, did little to help the coal companies. He admitted (as one newspaper wrote) that "a private government, whose army consists of the notorious 'mine guards,' exists in his state, and that though opposed to it, he is powerless to end it."

Within a few days, people began to sense that the State of West Virginia, rather than the miners, was on trial. "It looks as if the entire machinery of government has been turned over to the coal operators," another newspaper wrote.

While the coal companies tried to tie Blizzard and the organizers directly to the military action that took place on Blair Mountain, a principle witness was undermined when it turned out he was being paid by the coal companies. At one point in the trial, the prosecutor brought out a set of Springfield rifles to demonstrate the firepower of the miners. To show what the miners were up against, union lawyers brought out a diabolically constructed bomb dropped on the miners from a biplane. To boost the drama, the union asked experts to take it apart, there in the courtroom.

Day by day, Sunday by Sunday, and game by game, the jury and townsfolk began to see through the prosecution's portrait of the men as traitors who deserved execution. And as the coal industry's case fell apart, the people of Charles Town increasingly took the miner's side. Near the end of the trial, Blizzard's wife was seen entering the courtroom arm-in-arm with a jury member's wife.

On May 27, 1922, Bill Blizzard and fellow defendants were acquitted. "Cheers resounded throughout the courtroom," wrote William C. Blizzard. "Blizzard's mother, wife and children clung to his neck, while the young defendant, all smiles, shook hands with friends until his hand was sore."

In the end, no one was executed, but not all the other miners were acquitted. Some were sentenced to jail terms, but nearly all were paroled by 1925. And it wasn't all smooth sailing for the UMWA afterwards. Union membership dropped drastically in the 1920s, to the point where some historians maintain that the coal companies won the Battle of Blair Mountain.

Wess Harris, publisher of *When Miners March*, disagrees. "That's just a lot of hogwash," Harris said. "If anything, Blair Mountain was a victory. The twin events of Blair Mountain and the trials (at Charles Town) were the furnaces that forged the miners' steel that got them ready for the 1930s."

By then, new federal labor laws began to protect labor organizers.

Unions "struggle and lose, then struggle and win," William C. Blizzard wrote. What people need to understand was that there had always been something wrong with an industry that "produced a mint of wealth and forced its employees to live in poverty."

Other players on the first string included:

| | |
|---|---|
| Okey Johnson: Pitcher | Charge: Treason |
| Frank Stump: Catcher | Charge: Murder |
| Joe Rhodes: Shortstop | Charge: Murder |
| Dewey Bailey: Center field | Charge: Treason |
| A.C. McCormick: Left field | Charge: Murder |

Treason Trial

*Labor leader Bill Blizzard at bat in a baseball game, Charles Town, Jefferson County, 1922. Several members of the United Mine Workers were tried for treason following the Battle of Blair Mountain in Logan County during the Mine Wars. In a change of venue, the first trial was held in Charles Town. During the trial, union members, coal company officials and journalists played baseball. Incidentally, Blizzard was hit by a bat and injured just after this photo was taken. [William Blizzard Collection]*

## Union Miners Play Hardball.

This photo and the caption below it are both from *Picturing West Virginia*, published by the State Archives Division. Incredibly, in the State Museum at the capitol, along with this image state historians display an old softball as if it were a relic from that game.

The game orb in the June 16, 1963, edition of the *Charleston Gazette-Mail* is a true baseball which is currently on display with the *When Miners March* Traveling Museum. And despite what the caption below implies, Blizzard's team never played ball with the men who were trying to hang them!

# John L. Lewis: 40 Years of Upset Stomachs
## *Friend to Coal Miners, Tough Foe to Operators*
By William C. Blizzard

*The following article was originally published June 16, 1963, in the Charleston Newspapers'* Sunday Gazette-Mail.

For more than 40 years, from 1919 to 1960, John L. Lewis upset the stomach of the American public as that public absorbed the newspaper headlines with its breakfast. He not only was a friend of the miners, but during most of that time was the greatest friend the sodium bicarbonate manufacturers ever had.

Since Nov. 1, 1919, when Lewis, as acting president of the United Mine Workers of America, called his first nationwide strike of coal miners, the public has been reading these headlines: 'Government Moves to Stop Lewis;' 'Lewis Orders Work Stoppage;' 'Lewis Orders Miners Back;' 'Lewis Flays Coal Operators;' 'Lewis Defies Government Board;' and 'Lewis Wins Wage Increase.' Such headlines were typical for most of Lewis' 40 year tenure, as jonquils and coal miners came out of the ground together almost every spring.

Since his retirement in January, Lewis has been president emeritus of the UMW, has received an honorary doctorate from West Virginia University, and has been praised and feted by many of his former coal company enemies. The honors and praises may have been more prompted by relief than genuine respect or affection, but Lewis' adversaries had best not relax; for there is no reason to think that John L. Lewis' voice still may not ring strong and clear in UMW affairs, for all his 83 years.

During 40 years the names of Lewis and the UMW were synonymous. Except for brief internal opposition in the '20s and early '30s, John L. Lewis was the unchallenged leader of the coal diggers of the United States. His long tenure was not the result of chance, although neither was Lewis a tyrant who ruled his coal kingdom without the acquiescence of most of his miners.

That is, within the UMW the big bushy-browed man from Iowa built a machine not unlike any other political machine, and used it ruthlessly to perpetuate himself in office. How much the machine was needed may never be known, but on occasion it clipped off heads of opposition leaders like so many dandelions before the moving blade. On the other hand, Lewis was always, in an economic showdown, popular with the miners, and another leader of his stature was not on the scene during his reign.

Lewis has been called the Samson of the miners. As such, he was well aware that his strength lay in his union membership and its support, and that shorn of his miners he was as weak as any other man. He never forgot this, nor did he take chances of being scalped. For the miners every day touched the aorta of the nation, and if they wished temporarily to shut off the life of that nation, they were in a position to do so.

Lewis once explained this to Saul Alinsky, author of *John L. Lewis, An Unauthorized Biography* (Putman, 1949):

"When," said Lewis, "we control the production of coal we hold the vitals of our society right in our hands. I can squeeze, twist, and pull until we get the inevitable victory... Stop coal and you stop steel. Stop steel and you stop autos, and then tires and every part of our economy. Therefore, as a strike progresses, the hostility of the press and the government begins to build up pressure against us; but on the other hand the pressures for profits in steel and autos also develop and increase. The industrialists of autos and steel begin to apply pressure on the coal operators to accede to our demands, so that their own fabulous profits will not be interrupted. Thus we become the immovable anvil, with the operators relying on us being hammered into surrender by the pounding blows of steel, autos, (here Lewis laughed), and all other industrial allies, or accomplices, if you will."

In a way, this explanation of basic economic facts is the story of John L. Lewis' life. It takes toughness and durability to be an anvil, and both Lewis and his miners have had those qualities to a superlative degree. The union leader's description of his tactics is an excellent piece of writing, clear, graphic and accurate. But as the role of coal becomes less in our economy –and it is becoming less –this picture is changing, and a leader like Lewis will not be able so easily to paralyze the economy at will.

Nor will the coal miners be in so strong a bargaining position. But this is not the fault of Lewis, nor was automation in the coal fields brought on by him. For automation is a trend, with profit-making as its basis, which will ultimately affect every worker in the United States. The coal miner's plight is the prologue to a greater drama.

If you wish to know a great deal about John L. Lewis with minimum effort, you should read Saul Alinsky's book mentioned above. In toto, the book is pro-Lewis but it has profundity and lacks that reverence and servility which Alinsky describes as "reflected in the unhealthy awe that permeates every cranny and every stone of the UMW building in Washington, from its outside step to the ceiling of the sixth floor, and to that great Holy of Holies, where the union God abides."

No matter what his faults, which basically were arrogance and pride, John L. Lewis was the most able American labor leader of the past half century, and will retain that title until his death. If his great shadow killed off or withered other potential giants, it is the way of the towering oaks of human society just as it is the way of great oaks of the forest.

John Llewellyn Lewis was born in Lucas, Iowa, on Feb. 12 (Lincoln's birthday), 1880, the oldest son of a Welsh coal miner who was a member of the Knights of Labor. His father, Thomas, helped lead a strike in 1882 against the White Breast Fuel Co., a strike which was lost, leading to the blacklisting of Thomas as a union man too dangerous to hire.

Like many another man who has fought city hall in one guise or another, Thomas Lewis found the going hard, traveling from one area to another to secure work, losing jobs as the blacklist caught up with him. But in 1897 the blacklists were destroyed, and the Lewis family moved back to Lucas, where the father and two of his sons, one of them John, worked in the mines.

John L. Lewis never finished the eighth grade. But he liked to read and he liked to debate. Just under six feet and powerfully built, in his teens he organized both a debating team and a baseball team in Lucas. There he also met Myrta Edith Bell, daughter of a doctor from Ohio, of a family with strong cultural traditions. It was Miss Bell, who later became his wife, who encouraged John L. Lewis' love of reading, and guided him to the classics which later emerged in his public speeches.

But Lewis was not to marry his childhood sweetheart for some years. At 21, he left home and traveled throughout the West, hitching rides on freights when he had to, and working in many mines, digging for metal as well as coal. He was gone from Lucas for five years (Lewis has said: "I suppose if we talk about formal education I would count that five years as my education. It was a very important part of my life."), returning to Iowa and the coal mines in 1906.

By that time he had the basic qualities of a leader: the ability to speak well, a forceful physical appearance, aggressiveness, strong convictions and ambition. He ran for mayor of Lucas shortly after he married Myrta Bell in 1907 but was defeated. The local miners, however, sent him as a delegate to the national convention of the UMW that year.

Lewis was almost 30 when he moved to Panama, Ill., largely because he thought he had a better chance to make a showing as a labor leader in that area. Helped by his five brothers, who had also moved to Panama, he soon was elected local union president, then state legislative agent for the district UMW. It was in Illinois, after a pit disaster which killed 160 miners, that Lewis began his long career of separating politicians from their hides in order to gain benefits for the miners. His record before the Illinois Legislature brought Lewis to the attention of AFL President Samuel Gompers.

Gompers at the time needed a strong, tough man who also had brains, and in 1911 hired Lewis as a field representative and legislative agent for the American Federation of Labor. The big man from Lucas now was working as a union lobbyist and AFL organizer in the steel, lumber, glass, rubber and electrical industries, on a national level. From the age of about 31 to 37, he worked for the AFL, trying to organize the above named industries on a craft basis. He failed.

But he did not fail to advance himself within the UMW, of which he was yet a member, using his AFL position and expense account to build a personal machine within the miner's union. During the 1916 UMW national convention he served as UMW president pro tempore, and shortly afterward took a job as chief statistician for the UMW, resigning his AFL job.

Lewis had not failed to see the strategic role of the coal industry in the nation, and his failure to organize industries on a craft basis had taught him the value in mass industries, of the industrial-union approach of the UMW. In 1916, John L. Lewis moved with his family to Indianapolis, which was then national UMW head-quarters.

Lewis was on his way, but not even he could have anticipated how fast he was destined to move. In 1917, John P. White, seventh president of the UMW, resigned and was succeeded by Frank Hayes, who appointed Lewis vice president. Hayes had little interest in union affairs, liked the cup that cheers, and was mild-mannered and un-aggressive.

Lewis, it may be safely said, was neither mild nor unaggressive, and the UMW, as he could plainly see, was to be his life. Under Frank Hayes, he actually ran the UMW show, and in 1919 presided over the UMW national convention. In 1920, at the age of 40, he was elected president of the miners' union, a post he held for 40 years, or 10 years longer than the combined service of the eight UMW presidents who had preceded him.

John L. Lewis had arrived. Only 10 years before, or a little better, he had been a mere local union president at Panama, Ill.

Lewis was to call a nationwide strike, however, before he officially became the UMW chief. The war was over, and in the Fall of 1919 there were nearly 400,000 members in the UMW. World War I had produced the usual crop of war-making millionaires, while the coal miners had worked for $5 a day, pledged not only to not strike, but also to not ask for any change in wages or working conditions for the duration.

In 1919, with the war ended, UMW acting President Lewis called a strike for higher wages, a shorter work week, and a six-hour day, to begin Nov.1, 1919. The government insisted that the war was technically still on, although shooting had stopped a year before, and Woodrow Wilson, an enemy of labor, forbade the strike.

The miners went out Nov.1, just the same, defying a federal court injunction. Lewis and 84 union officials were cited for contempt. On Dec.7, Lewis called off the strike, defeated by Woodrow Wilson and the federal courts. But the miners did receive an immediate small increase through Lewis' agreement with Wilson, and another larger increase from an appointed commission a little later.

John L. Lewis had led his first national strike, and all had not gone so well. There is evidence that the coal miners were considerably more militant than their chief at that time, and that the UMW convention which greeted Lewis after he called off the strike was hostile. The convention ratified his actions and agreement only by the use of the existing, but yet weak, Lewis machine.

Lewis learned much from the 1919 struggle, the principal lesson being that it was both uncomfortable and inconvenient to face a large room full of hostile coal miners who could, if sufficiently aroused, fire you from your job. Lewis determined to see to it that the UMW became a unified force which would back his orders and give him job security. That is, he built a machine, a good heavy one that would iron out threats to his rule.

At the same time that such a machine secured Lewis' personal position, it also insured that 400,000 coal miners would act as a unit, so that their strength might be felt. Lewis looked upon himself as a commander-in-chief, and he knew that only with a disciplined army could victories be won. The army of miners became an extension of his will, just as any army is the extension and implement of the will of any general. It remained that for 40 years.

He assured his control of the UMW by revoking autonomy in the union districts in the coal states. That is, top UMW district officials were elected by their membership before the Lewis reign, but were appointed by Lewis not many years after he took office. If they supported his policies, he retained them; if they opposed him, he fired them, replacing them with his own men. The Lewis men heading the districts then enforced Lewis policies in their respective areas.

This was not, in some cases, easily done, but done it was. Lewis ran against Sam Gompers in 1921 for presidency of the AFL, but was beaten two to one when the votes were counted. Some UMW district leaders who didn't like Lewis helped in his defeat, and also fought his national UMW leadership.

Principal among them were Frank Farrington of Illinois and Alex Howat of Kansas. Charles A. Madison, in "American Labor Leaders" (Harper, 1950), states flatly that when John Brophy, president of UMW District 2 in Pennsylvania, ran against Lewis for the UMW presidency in 1926, he was "counted out by machine tactics" (Many years later, however, Lewis appointed Brophy to the post of executive director of the new-born CIO.).

Lewis tactics at UMW conventions are described by Saul Alinsky: "At one of the conventions, Alex Howat made his customary Pickett's charge down the center aisle and up onto the platform. Then came the usual aftermath as Howat was seized and sent sailing through the air and into the audience and Lewis' followers on the platform panted from the exertion necessary from this feat. Howat's demands for recognition by Chairman Lewis were denied and the convention began to shout and hiss and boo its disapproval. Lewis calmly regarded the bedlam for some moments and then boomed, 'May the chair state that you may shout until you meet each other in hell and he will not change his ruling.'"

There were Socialists and Communists in the UMW at that time, and Lewis disliked them as much as they disliked him. He had prepared a series of articles on the Red menace, at UMW expense, which were widely circulated in newspaper and magazines. In the articles, he asserted, in essence, that all radicals and many liberals were agents of Moscow, and that many UMW troubles arose from their treasonous activity.

In his effort to defeat all comers, Lewis pulled out all stops and used all tactics which he hoped might be effective. The ethics of the matter were seldom, if ever, considered, just as they seldom are by practical and ambitious men in any line of endeavor. The criterion of any tactic apparently was "Will it work?"

Using this same criterion, for instance, Lewis in his CIO days (1935-1940), forgot his former hatred of leftists. During the early days of the CIO, Lewis needed help in the organization of mass industries. He needed organizers who were intelligent, fearless, and possessed of missionary zeal. Among Communists and other radicals he found these qualities, and he did not hesitate to hire them. John Brophy and Powers Hapgood, for instance, were hired, and placed in top positions in the CIO. Neither was a Communist but both were critics of capitalism and favored some sort of Socialist society.

In addition, both had fought Lewis in the UMW, and sharp blows had been exchanged. Nevertheless, Lewis hired them to rock the cradle of his brainchild, the CIO, and they proved able babysitters, in more ways than one as Goodyear and General Motors were to learn. All along the line Lewis hired CIO personnel who could do the job best, and did not, as he put it, "turn them upside down to see what sort of literature fell out of their pockets."

Such radicals spearheaded the CIO drive, although it should be emphasized that they in no way originated or managed the CIO. That responsibility belonged to Lewis. The fact that most of them were later ejected from that organization is the sort of irony that history seems fond of.

The early years of Lewis leadership were not happy ones for the UMW, which shrank from a membership of more than 425,000 in 1921 to less than 150,000 in 1932. Part of this may have been Lewis' fault, as his critics claimed, but much of this withering was caused by the economics of the coal industry, plus the economic and political power of big business prior to 1929.

Coal was so plentiful that what the coal miner was bringing to the surface was not bringing much of a price. There were too many coal mines and coal miners, all fiercely competing with one another, supplying too much coal to a glutted market. A union leader does not, under such conditions, find it easy or even possible to keep wages rising, and if a union does not do that its membership drifts away.

The debacle of 1929 made matters worse. Then came the U.S. election year of 1932, with Herbert Hoover opposing Franklin D. Roosevelt. Lewis favored Hoover, partly because the Norris-LaGuardia Act was passed during his tenure, and in part possibly because of early bias toward the Republican party. But when Roosevelt took office, and Lewis was able to get Section 7A of the

National Industry Recovery Act into law, the mine union leader immediately supported Roosevelt.

This famous Section 7A, which affirmed the right of workers to join a union of their choice, was the work of John L. Lewis, and led to the rebirth of the UMW in the early '30s and the founding and success of the CIO.

John L. Lewis has fought hard for both Republican and Democratic candidates, but he explained his political beliefs at the National Press Club in 1936: "I am not a Republican. I am not a Democrat. I am not a Fascist, Communist, or a Socialist."

What political party, you might ask, does this leave? It leaves none, actually, for Lewis has always been for the politician who was for him, for the UMW, and for labor, and he felt that all three of these were a united trinity. This has been the key to Lewis' politics, although he seldom found a politician in that category.

If a politician really wasn't in that category, however, Lewis often made a counterfeit labor sympathizer do just as well. And there were lots of them. Franklin Roosevelt was such a counterfeit, according to Lewis.

According to Lewis, Roosevelt actually fought the enactment of Section 7A. But Lewis did not tell the coal miners of this Roosevelt attitude, and he knew FDR was publicly proclaiming sympathy for labor. So Lewis sent his organizers into the coal fields, pointing to Section 7A and saying: "President Roosevelt wants you to join the union!"

Roosevelt, of course, had said no such thing, but Lewis knew that FDR, for political reasons, was not likely to deny it. By late 1933, UMW membership had risen to more than 500,000, and the CIO was a gleam in John L. Lewis' eye. He argued the merits of industrial versus craft unionism with top AFL leaders, but met a stone wall. Although William Green had been a coal miner and secretary treasurer of the UMW at one time, and was yet a UMW member, he and his executive council in 1935 turned down the Lewis offer to help "organize the unorganized" (Saul Alinsky credits this slogan to Lewis, but it was coined by John Brophy, or at least appeared in print under his byline, as early as 1926).

Then Lewis and the heads of seven AFL craft unions met and formed the Committee (later the Congress) for Industrial Organization. Lewis himself was still an AFL vice president, but resigned his post in late 1935. In August 1936, the AFL ejected the CIO unions, charging dual unionism. The UMW also was ejected, and Lewis retaliated by ousting William Green from his original union.

There is no space here to detail the CIO organizing drive in rubber, steel, and other industries. Lewis gave about three-quarters of a million dollars to the second Roosevelt campaign, and FDR captured all but eight of the nation's 531 electoral votes. But in 1937, during the General Motors "sit-down" strike, Lewis began to mistrust Roosevelt, who apparently told the labor leader he favored the sit-downs and Michigan Gov. Frank Murphy just the opposite.

Lewis expected a friendly Roosevelt because of the large amount of money donated to his 1936 campaign. And Lewis became convinced that not only was Roosevelt unfriendly, but was stabbing him in the back.

When he discovered, through Frank Murphy, that Roosevelt had his telephones tapped by the FBI, at his office and at home, and that he was under surveillance by J. Edgar Hoover, Lewis was understandably miffed.

On Oct 25, 1940, the UMW head made his famous radio speech in which he opposed Roosevelt for re-election and threatened to resign from the CIO if FDR were elected. Roosevelt was elected for a third term, and Lewis kept his word. That this was a tragedy for the CIO, the UMW and the entire labor movement seems with hindsight, painfully evident.

Some of Lewis' old UMW cohorts, like Van Bittner and Phillip Murray, broke with Lewis, or were booted by him from the UMW when they persisted in supporting Roosevelt. In October, 1941, Lewis took the UMW from the CIO. The latter organization split into warring factions within a few years, then united with the AFL. Lewis went back into the AFL for a time but took his miners out again. Today, as has been true for several years, the labor movement is badly divided, snubbed by politicians and hamstrung by the Taft-Hartley Act and other restrictive legislation.

It is true that for some years Lewis had considered the establishment of a third major political party with a farmer-laborer base. But he knew that such a party could succeed, possibly by taking over the Democratic party, only with the support of an organized, unified, labor movement. If Lewis had remained with the CIO, such a huge, unified movement might have been possible under his leadership. That a third party was not possible without a mighty labor base was demonstrated by the Progressive party fiasco in 1948.

But as Lewis has pointed out, speculation on what might have been is futile. He went on to fight Roosevelt during the war against Germany and Japan, in 1943 calling out his miners three times (after a preliminary spontaneous walkout) in protest against the "little steel formula" which had the effect of freezing wages. Lewis won increases for the miners including a welfare and retirement fund, but he also reaped vilification on an unprecedented scale.

Lewis was cursed by the left, the right, and the man on the street for striking his miners during World War II. But he knew what he was doing, from a tactical point of view, and the coal miners followed his orders in an impressive show of solidarity and loyalty. They were fighting a sort of war underground, and it is interesting to know that the coal miners in the course of their work from 1941 through 1945 lost 6,561 killed and 322,873 wounded.

In the years before his retirement, Lewis concentrated upon improving the miners' welfare and retirement program, until the royalty which financed it reached 40 cents a ton, and he built 10 hospitals in West Virginia and Kentucky. From a public relations and humanitarian point of view, nothing he ever did surpassed this program.

What Lewis had done for his miners in other ways, however, was not only impressive but almost incredible. During the period 1935 to 1939, among 15 major basic industries the average wage of coal miners was third from the bottom. Ten years later, Lewis had increased that wage by 246.8 percent, and wages of coal miners led all the rest.

Lewis retired from the UMW leadership in 1960, and is now the union's president emeritus. Whether another Lewis is now developing to cope with modern problems is unknown, but none is now visible. There are problems. Automation has reduced coal mine employees to about 136,0000, and the Welfare Fund is threatened. Four of the union hospitals may be forced to close.

John L. Lewis was and is a complex man, and the final story about him and his role in the labor movement has not been written. But the importance of his role is not to be doubted. Perhaps it is well that Samson of labor is stepping out of the picture at a time when his strength is being shorn away by automation.

Whatever the verdict of history, another such man is not likely soon to appear on the national scene.

\*\*\*\*\*\*\*\*\*\*\*\*\*\*\*\*\*\*\*\*\*\*\*\*\*\*\*\*\*\*\*\*\*\*\*\*\*\*\*\*\*\*

*"If we must grind up human flesh and bone in the industrial machine that we call modern America, then before God, I assert that those who consume the coal, and you and I who benefit from that service because we live in comfort, we owe protection to those men first, and we owe the security for their family if they die. I say it, I voice it, I proclaim it, and I care not who in heaven or hell opposes it!"*    —John Llewlyn Lewis

February 12, 1880 – June 11, 1969

Union Miners
Carbondale mine
July, 1926

Gem Photo

Courtesy of The George Bragg Collection

Coal Owner's Union
Atlantic City
July, 1923

Journalist William C. Blizzard was proud into his 9th decade that as a youth he had achieved the rank of Eagle Scout. His father, Bill, had actively encouraged the Boy Scouts of America to become involved in the early coal camps.

Official historians for the State of West Virginia persist in labeling Bill an "ardent socialist."

*Photo courtesy of the Radford University Archives*
*William C. Blizzard/ When Miners March Collection*

# Even heroes gotta fish.

Bill Blizzard relaxes outside his home
in Winfield, WV.

*Photo courtesy of the Radford University Archives,*
*William C. Blizzard/ When Miners March Collection*

Apprentice archeologists Jesse and Wesley Daniels join mentor Brandon Nida at his Whipple Company Store dig site.

William C. Blizzard, Wess Harris and students from Xavier University share the picket line with miners from Local 8843.

*Photo courtesy of the When Miners March Traveling Museum Collection*

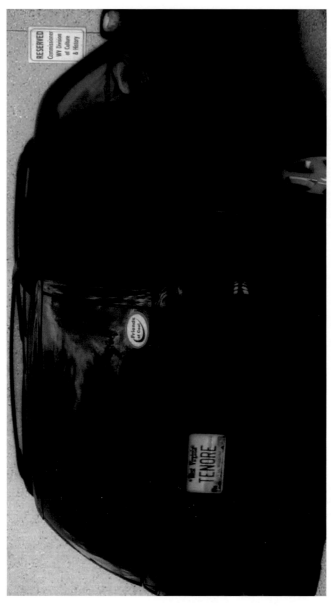

Parked in the spot reserved for the Commissioner of the WV Division of Culture and History bearing Randall Reid-Smith's unique vanity plate, his vehicle also displays another passion. The Friends of Coal logo on his window is the registered trademark of the West Virginia Coal Association.

photo by Wess Harris

Photo Credit: MSHA

UBB rock-dusting machine pictured where it was found outside the mine. "When MSHA put power on the machine to test it as part of the investigation, the motor burned up."

Source: *INDUSTRIAL HOMICIDE: Report on the Upper Big Branch Mine Disaster.* (UMWA)

The well rock dusted mine cannot explode. Safe, legal coal mines are white, not black.

*Photo by Wess Harris*

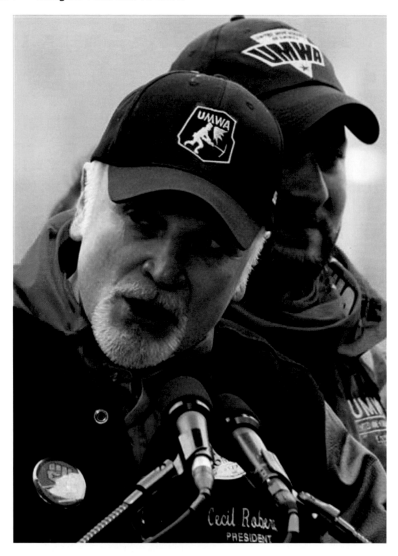

## Cecil Roberts, President of the United Mine Workers of America
*photo credit Charleston Gazette*

**United Mine Workers of America**

CECIL E. ROBERTS
INTERNATIONAL PRESIDENT

TELEPHONE
(703) 291-2420
FAX (703) 291-2451

UNITED MINE WORKERS' HEADQUARTERS
18354 QUANTICO GATEWAY DRIVE, SUITE 200
**Triangle, VA**
22172-1779

July 26, 2011

Mr. Randall Reid-Smith, Commissioner
WV Division of Culture and History
The Culture Center
1900 Kanawha Blvd., East
Charleston, WV 25305

Dear Mr. Reid-Smith,

Shortly after the opening of the West Virginia State Museum, it was brought to my attention that there are a series of inaccuracies in the description of the UMWA, UMWA personnel and coal miners' history in the museum's displays. Additionally, I have received many complaints about the overall impression a visitor receives of the UMWA's role in West Virginia's history, life in the company towns, the events leading up to the Battle of Blair Mountain, the battle itself and other aspects of the displays in the museum.

Over the past months, several members of the UMWA staff have visited the West Virginia State Museum on many separate occasions. I have been to the museum myself, and seen the displays there. I have a number of very serious concerns with what is an inaccurate portrayal of the UMWA and our history of oppression and struggle against the coal operators of the 19th and 20th centuries.

The UMWA's concerns with the museum's displays are not only about the factual inaccuracies, but also extend to numerous misleading statements and lack of full information provided in the exhibits.

Let me start with this: There are two completely inaccurate statements in the museum's displays that I would like to see changed immediately:

- On "The Failure of Violence" plaque, the museum's text says that Bill Blizzard became the President of "Local" 17 of the UMWA. In fact, he became President of District 17, not Local 17. A local union is operational at only one workplace. A District encompasses all the local unions within a geographical area, in this case, southern West Virginia.

- On the "Bill Blizzard" plaque, the same mistake is made. Raymond Lewis became District 17 President, not Local 17. We also have concerns about the statement that Bill Blizzard resigned because John L. Lewis demoted him solely in order to put his brother in Blizzard's place.

Beyond these outright mistakes, there are a host of misleading statements, biases, and incomplete information in almost every exhibition concerning coal miners, life in the coal camps, and more.

Specifically, the following "rooms" in the museum contain displays that are objectionable and do not present the actual history of these things anywhere near what it actually was:

- The "Company Store," including the discussion of the system of using mine company scrip instead of U.S. legal tender to pay miners. Your presentation makes it seem as if the scrip system was little different from a credit card, where miners and their families could pay off expensive purchases over time.

Nowhere is it mentioned that miners had absolutely no choice as to whether they used scrip or not. Nowhere is it mentioned that going somewhere else instead of the company store to purchase goods and equipment was an offense frequently punishable by a beating from the company's Baldwin-Felts thugs followed by dismissal from employment and eviction from the company house.

- "Coal mining," including misleading statements regarding Island Creek Coal and UMWA organizing, as well as a very small presentation regarding the worst industrial disaster in United States history – the explosion at the Monongah mine – that includes language regarding the company's Christmas "gift" to the families of those killed that is offensive to the memories of the fallen miners.

- "The Battle of Blair Mountain," which blames Sid Hatfield for instigating the violence in the coalfields that led to that battle, instead of focusing on the daily violence inflicted on coal miners and their families in the coal camps of the day.

The film you show about Blair Mountain and accompanying panels also say that Bill Blizzard and others who were tried in the aftermath of the Battle were charged with treason against the United States, when in fact they were charged with treason against the state of West Virginia. As I'm sure you know, one cannot be treasonous against a single state, one can only be treasonous against all the United States. You fail to point this out, thereby perpetuating the false notion that these men were not true Americans.

There are several other issues with these and other displays that the UMWA finds objectionable, misleading, and biased; and which we are willing to discuss with you and your staff.

It is, to say the least, disappointing to find that what is supposed to be an authoritative presentation on our state's unique history – and one that surely costs West Virginia taxpayers millions of dollars to build and maintain – contains inaccurate, false, misleading and biased presentations.

Indeed, in just about every instance where the UWMA is mentioned in the museum, we are linked with violence or some other unsavory activity. There is no mention of the millions of West Virginians who have, over the past 60+ years, received and continue to receive the benefits of UMWA pensions and retiree health care – considerably easing their senior years – which were negotiated by the UMWA.

There is no mention of the UMWA's leading role in passing mine safety and health legislation which have saved countless lives in West Virginia and throughout the nation. There is no mention of the UMWA's role in fighting to end black lung and to establish and then protect black lung compensation.

Instead, the impression a visitor with little or no knowledge of the history of the coal industry and the UMWA would take away from the museum is that the union is made up of people who, while perhaps willing to work hard, are just as willing to be prone to armed violence to settle our problems, be they internal or external.

It is said that the "victors write history." I would point out that the fight between coal miners, our families and our communities against those who would exploit us is far from over. We have no intention of allowing a twisted version of what life was really like for our ancestors and ourselves to be foisted on an unsuspecting public.

I look forward to hearing from you as to how soon you intend to correct the false information contained in the museum, and whether or not you intend to work with the UMWA on correcting the biases imparted by so many of the museum's displays.

Sincerely,

Cecil E. Roberts

cc:     Hon. Earl Ray Tomblin, Governor
        Hon. Jay Rockefeller, United States Senator
        Hon. Nick Rahall, Member of Congress
        Hon. Kay Huffman Goodwin, Secretary, Department of Education and the Arts
        Hon. Jeffrey Kessler, Acting President of the Senate
        Hon. Rick Thompson, Speaker of the House
        Hon. Mike Caputo, Majority Whip
        Joe Carter, UMWA International District 17 Vice President
        Gary Trout, UMWA Region IV Director
        Ted Hapney, UMWA Eastern COMPAC Director
        Marty Hudson, Executive Assistant to the UMWA President
        Bob Scaramozzino, Administrator, UMWA President's Office
        Phil Smith, UMWA Director of Communications
        Emily Smith, UMWA Archivist/Collection Manager
        Paul Nyden, Charleston Gazette
        Ken Ward, Charleston Gazette

# The New York Times

# DRUMHEAD LAW RULED COAL CAMPS

---

## West Virginia Militia Officers Describe Star-Chamber Trials of Miners.

---

## ALL CIVIL COURTS IGNORED

---

## Senators Satisfied Citizens Were Convicted in Violation of Federal Constitution.

*Published June 12, 1913*

# Cecil Roberts Shares His Story
Michael Kline

I read and re-read the words of Cecil Roberts with blurred excitement. The idea that the leader of the United Mine Workers would go public with his critique of the "Coal" exhibit at the West Virginia State Museum gave me hope. In the current political climate in Charleston, our governors, judges and legislative leaders still dance to the beat of Don Blankenship's drum. "We are the extractive state," they proclaim, "and we are open for business." Never mind that the major proceeds of this business are leaving the State. The profits go elsewhere and always have, leaving our citizens deprived and demoralized. In this oppressive atmosphere of intense lobbying and rising corporate profits we have seen few signs of hope on the horizon, hope for more recognition of the lives our forebears lived under the whip lash of company rule, hope for an unveiling of a more accurate accounting of our industrial culture and Union organizing history than as it is currently portrayed in State exhibits and publications. The Roberts letter above is one of those signs. It is a sign that authentic interpretations of coal field life and memory will prevail, despite apparent sustained efforts to suppress and sanitize them. Our grandchildren will take an interest in how the "grands" came through it all. They will stand a little taller.

In the early fall of 2011, President Roberts agreed to sit for a recorded interview exploring issues of labor history in the arenas of public culture and history. We met at the headquarters of the United Mine Workers of America in Triangle, Virginia. Carrie Kline joined me in this documentary opportunity as did Phil Smith, Director of Communications for the Union. The Headquarters' hallways are hung with haunting and historically significant photos alongside glass cases laden with artifacts and documents tracing early developments in Union history. We could have spent days trying to absorb this extensive exhibit. Here is an organization that has gone to great lengths to preserve and present its past with vivid accessibility. Our brief tour before the interview felt like an invitation to come inside the story. Once seated with Roberts around a table in the executive office, we could not imagine what sort of a story it would be. But we always begin our interviews with the same question.

**Michael Kline:** Tell me about your people and where you were raised.

**Cecil Roberts:** "I was born in Kayford, West Virginia. You go 15 miles up Cabin Creek Road and then the black top runs out. And then you turn to the right on a dirt road called Shamrock Hollow. And I was born in a company house there in 1946 and delivered by a company doctor and in the company house. We were all raised in the company house, company town, lived there on Cabin Creek all my life until I was elected to come here. I went straight from Cabin Creek to Washington DC, which is a little bit of a difference (laughing) in culture, among other things, yes.

"You might be amazed by how many people lived in Kayford at that time. People used to actually fight over ----. When someone moved out of a company house, and people knew someone was moving, you'd go to the company store and you'd sign a list and say I want to be considered for Phil Smith's house when he moves out. But the superintendent of the company store made that determination of who got to live in what house.

Everywhere you looked there was a house, and there wasn't an empty house to be seen anywhere back up in those hollows. All the company houses I lived in weren't identical but they were very close to it.

"Coal mining in those days was—this is before mechanization had really taken a stronghold—miners were mostly hand-loading back in the '40s and '50s. And my earliest recollection is that coal miners were everywhere."

## MECHANIZATION

**Roberts:** "The UMWA was the largest union in the country in the '30s. We were over 800,000 members, and that held true for a while. And then mechanization came along. The first wave of mechanization was probably around the early '50s. There had been some of that in the late '40s but it really hit hard in the '50s when (UMWA President) John L. Lewis pretty much accepted mechanization, that it was inevitable. You weren't going to stop companies from being able to mine coal with loading machines, and cutting machines, shuttle cars. And so a lot of people lost their jobs. They were hand-loaders. The UMWA sometime in the early '50s lost like 300,000 members, all in a matter of a few years after signing the contract that created the Health and Retirement Funds in the late '40s. So by the time I was born, the Union was changing dramatically, coal mining was changing dramatically, and it really changed by the mid '50s and in a very profound way.

"I guess we saw the first wave of real unemployment hit hard in the coal fields in those days. A lot of people left the coal fields and made their way to places like Cleveland, Ohio, Detroit, Michigan, and Flint, Michigan, to go to work in the auto factories, and the steel mills of Pittsburgh and other places. So a lot of people migrated from West Virginia and Kentucky out of the coal fields to other areas of the country. That's why you find so many people who tell you, 'My grandfather was a coal miner or my great-grandfather.' That is all true because we had 800,000 people mining coal in 1938, '39, '40 and down to probably 500,000 mining coal by the mid '50s. So where did all those people go? Well they left and they took their kids with them and most of them had four, five, six kids. Some of them had ten kids, and then they all had kids and they all had kids. And you hear those stories wherever you go. My recollection is that when we got into the '60s, we began to see lots of layoffs, not because of mechanization per say, but because the demand for coal was down. From about 1960 up until about 1970 almost no one was hired in the coal industry. If people were working in the coal industry in 1960, they might have had jobs throughout the '60s, but there wasn't this mass attempt to hire people."

## MORE CHANGES

**Roberts:** "Of course, that changed in 1970, '71. If you remember around the time of the 1973 Arab oil embargo, literally thousands of young people were hired in the industry. And I was one of them. Those people who were hired were a little different. I was a Vietnam veteran. Lots of Vietnam veterans were hired. Many of those young people who went in the mines with me had some college backgrounds. Some had a little more extensive education than perhaps those who were working in the mines at that time. So you had this great conflict between the older miners who were in their 50s and younger miners in their 20s. Two different kinds of thinking about the way things ought to be done. When a foreman would ask a young person to do something that he thought was dangerous, he's not doing it. And then you had a lot of wildcat strikes, a lot of turmoil about that same time. And we had the Farmington disaster in 1968. Tony Boyle went down after the Farmington disaster and praised the company. And they had just had an explosion that killed 78 men. So you had all those things that came together. This was not only in the coal industry but within the union itself. Down in the southern part of the state the black-lung movement was ongoing. It was very much a rank and file movement. You had a handful of doctors, maybe a couple of lawyers supporting that effort.

"The union for the most part wasn't supporting that. And you had this clash between the rank and file and the establishment in the union led by Tony Boyle and others. On the other hand, you had this effort by Jock Yablonsky who had run (for the presidency of the Union) on a platform of autonomy and democracy. He lost the election and then lost his life. And then you had Miners for Democracy, so you had all that turmoil within the union coming between 1968 and 1972. That was about the most significant four years that I can point to as far as changes within the movement itself, and yet when Arnold Miller got elected he brought democracy to the union and people like me had an opportunity to run for office. And if it wasn't for Jock Yablonski and Arnold Miller, maybe I wouldn't be sitting here talking to you. I might be pumping gas somewhere down around Chelyan or Cabin Creek or somewhere. But they opened doors and many of us were ready to walk through. That would include Rich Trumka, myself, and many other young people at that time. We took advantage of the autonomy and ran for office and got elected."

## FARMINGTON BLOOD BRINGS NEW LAWS

**Roberts:** "So, within those four years, you had a passage of the first federal legislation to protect coal miners: 1969 Coal Mine Health and Safety Act, which included for the first time the recognition of pneumoconiosis as an occupational disease. And with the explosion at Farmington (came a new level of public awareness), with people watching on television—not just in the coal fields but in Los Angeles, Florida, New York City—watching the mine explode and then explode again, watching interviews with the widows. I think television might have played a huge role in bringing about the federal legislation to protect coal miners because it was not just something confined to Cabin Creek and Paint Creek and places like that. It was like the whole nation watched. So I've always said that the 78 miners who lost their lives in Farmington were kind of like heroes on a battlefield, that they gave their lives for everyone else."

"If you look at statistics of the 1969 Coal Mine Health and Safety Act, 40 years before the passage of the act, 30,000 miners lost their lives mining coal in the nation. Forty years afterwards, it was less than 3,000. The passage of that act saved many lives. I think the tragedy of this is that we didn't pass this legislation sooner. We've had worse coal mine accidents and explosions. You had Centralia in Illinois, where hundreds lost their lives. Nothing happened. It was in the early '50s. You had another explosion at West Frankfort, and over 100 miners lost their lives. Nothing happened legislatively. It took a tragedy like Farmington that everyone watched for the changes to come about."

## THE BLACK LUNG TOLL

"Then you think about the hundreds of thousands of people who suffered from pneumoconiosis and never received benefits or even had the fact (established) that such disease existed. 1969 was the first time the country acknowledged that pneumoconiosis was an occupational illness. I think that's tragic in and of itself. So I think 1968 to 1972 is a significant time. You can look backward from there, and you can look forward from there to see how coal mining has been dealt with. I mean, it took, I guess, close to a hundred years [after the birth of the coal mining industry] to have health and safety laws passed by the Congress, and it took the same amount of time to recognize black-lung as a disease. Miners used to call it 'miners asthma.' They knew they were sick and they figured they got sick from mining coal, but no one could tell them, or would tell them what was wrong with them. Miners used to choke to death and never be compensated a dime for it. Miners died at a very young age. So one of the tragedies I think of the coal fields is a failure to protect miners until very recently. We went the vast majority of the time without any protection for coal miners either health-wise or safety-wise. There's been over 100,000 coal miners killed in this nation's mines. In addition over 100,000 have died from black lung. So we've got over 200,000 miners who lost their lives and most of those lives have been lost without any protection from the government. And I think that's one of the sad stories of coal mining in the United States of America."

"But I guess the good news is that we did pass legislation in 1969. We built on that. And miners mining today are safer. They minc coal with a longwall as opposed to a shovel. Mining is not quite the backbreaking work it once was. And we have recognized black lung as an occupational illness, although I do think it is tragic that we don't compensate more miners than we do. I mean, probably around 12 to 14% of those people who apply for the benefits now receive them. Not long ago, it was only 7% receiving benefits. But every miner walking in applying for black lung benefits a few years back would get them. So there is a tragic story here about health and safety that we all can look back on and talk about how we could've done things a lot better."

## TWO HOUSES FOR $100

**Roberts:** "Then we can spin backward to the period of my youth, from my birth in 1946 to 1969. And using that as a benchmark, for the most part, up until the '60s coal miners were still living in coal company houses and still going to the company store. And there is no shame in moving into a–. I never saw anything wrong with living in a company house, but I think the fact that miners didn't have the flexibility to buy their own homes is something to speak to here. My Dad built our house. He bought a property back in the '50s and then over a three year period built his own home on Cabin Creek at a place called Dawes. My Mom and Dad would get their mail in Miami on Cabin Creek, so we were kind of right on the border of Miami and Dawes. We had to move from a company house at Kayford to a company house at Acme because they were putting in an overhead belt line over the top of the houses where we lived in Kayford. And then they sold us our house for $50 and we bought the house next to us for $50. So Daddy bought two houses for $100 but we had to tear them down and move them out. He took materials from the two houses we bought to build the house that my mother lives in now. You can go down the basement and see the old black two-by-twelves Dad used for the sub-flooring. You can go up in the attic and see the old two-by-fours. And they're real dark and rough cut. But we took the lumber out of those two company houses to built the house at Dawes and I helped him tear those houses down. I was about 11 years old then and helped him some with the building. It took him about three years. He built that house by hand with the help of his brother, my uncle. And an old, retired carpenter lived close by; he'd come over and help. That house has a special place for all of us because Daddy built it with his hands."

**Kline:** And, and he was working in mines all of this times?

**Roberts:** "Yes, he was."

**Kline:** What was his name?

**Roberts:** "Same as mine. Cecil Roberts. He –I think Dad might have been about sixteen when he started work in the mines. He went in with my grandfather. I never met either one of my grandfathers. They were both killed in the mines before I was born. Dad's father's name was Robert Roberts and he took Dad in the mines with him. And then when he was killed, Daddy kind of became the head of the household. He had two younger brothers at home and he had to help to raise them, help my grandmother. And then my grandfather on my mother's side, he also was killed in the mines. Both of them were killed by slate falls on Cabin Creek. So I've never had the benefit of grandfathers to talk to or hear stories from. And both, like I said, they both were killed in mines.

## BEST HEALTH CARE IN THE WORLD

**Roberts:** "The mines, you know, the mines have taken a lot of good men over many, many years. Of course, miners have made really good wages and benefits over the years and had excellent health care for the most of their lives as a result of what Lewis did in 1946 and '47. Pension plans have been fairly decent. It's not provided benefits to miners at a level that they could—until recently—support their families on once they retired. We've done pretty well in the last 10 or 15 years with respect to that. We've been able to raise benefits for miners who retired recently. But we take great pride in the fact that we have some of the best healthcare in the world and have had that since 1946. And it's been a fight to keep it, but we're proud that we still have it.

"So it's been a lot of pain and suffering in the coal fields. And the fact that when people get killed one or two at time it doesn't draw the attention that a Sago or an Upper Big Branch might receive, or with respect to Farmington. But more miners have been killed one or two at a time than at (much larger disasters). A lot of miners have been killed by slate falls, maybe electrocuted, run over by equipment, and those tragedies are just as painful and hurtful to families as those that grab the news and receive all the attention on TV. Those families hurt just as bad as the other families hurt. A lot of tragedies and a lot of pain and suffering goes with coal mining, but it is an honorable profession. I'm proud that I came from a coal mining family and proud that I'm a coal miner myself."

# SCHOOL DAYS:  GOOD TIMES, HARD TIMES

**Kline:** Can you talk about what was like to be a kid growing up at that time and your schooling?

**Roberts:** "Sure. I went to the Kayford Elementary School. It doesn't exist any more, but I went there until I was in the Third Grade. That's when we moved down to Acme. I went from the Third Grade to the Sixth Grade at Acme Elementary School. A minister there from one of the Methodist churches, Cecil Burns, was the principal at Acme. I still remember him very well. I remember going to the Kayford Company Store to shop, and in fact was probably the one that painted the store the last time it was painted, when I was seventeen years of age. That was my first job, painting some company stores when I was seventeen. I got very wealthy doing it, $1.25 an hour, I think that's what I was getting for it. That was minimum wage back in those days. I went to school everyday, had good friends and good teachers.

"I guess some people might look at us and say we were poor, but I didn't know that. I mean, you just know what surrounds you, right?"

**Kline:** And your play mates, the kids that you knew around Cabin Creek? They were all pretty healthy?

**Roberts:** "Yes, all the kids that I played with were coal miners' sons and daughters. People forget how many folks lived in those coal camps back then.

"We never wanted for anything even when Dad would be laid off in the '60s. A lot of layoffs occurred in the late '50s and throughout the '60s. Dad was unemployed for about three years in the coal fields. And he left and went to Ohio to work for a while, then he came back and got a job in the mines again on Cabin Creek. So we had times when Dad was not working very regularly. That was tough."

**Kline:** Did you go to Ohio with him at that point?

**Roberts:** "No, Mom and the kids stayed home. And Dad stayed with his brother and worked at building these huge shovels in one of the factories out in, I think, Marion, Ohio. And he was, like I said, he was in and out for about three years. He'd come home or we'd go out to see him. We'd go out there at Christmas time or whatever so we could stay together. And then when he had a chance to get a job back in the mines, he took it. And Dad was able to work up until the time Bethlehem Steel shut down at Kayford. And I think they announced the closure in 79. He worked there up until about March of 1980. And I thought Dad would never enjoy retirement but I don't think anyone ever enjoyed retirement more than he did."

**Kline:** What do you mean?

**Roberts:** "Well, he just, you know, he was always on the midnight shift. So Dad would sleep during the day. He was a Union fire boss. So he had to go out to work early in order to inspect a mine before anyone else would go in. And he worked, worked, worked, worked, and slept in the daytime when he was in the mines. And then I thought, oh gee, he'll never enjoy retirement. All he's ever done is work. But he enjoyed it once he retired. He and my mother would spend time together. They'd go down–. Everywhere my mother went Dad went. Mom used to joke about that and said, "Your Dad never went anywhere with me, but now I can't go anywhere without him." And then they'd go to eat, go to shop, and do things together. They were married 68 years. And I used to joke with Dad. I talked to them both at the same time on the phone. On their anniversary I'd say "Dad, I think this is going to work out." And he said, "I don't know if it is or not." (Laughter). He was joking. He had a great sense of humor. He was a great storyteller. My Dad remembered that—. He could tell you about when he was five years old. He remembered that Blair Mountain March. Oh, yeah."

**Kline:** What did he say about that?

**Roberts:** "He said that all the men were gone and only the women and kids were left. And they, I think they might have been living in a tent at that time over on Seng Creek. And he said everyone was scared to death because they didn't know if their husbands or fathers were coming back or not. They knew the men were marching to Logan. He remembered. He used to tell this as though it happened yesterday. He said, 'We were all standing—. All the women were gathered up talking and had all of their kids close by. There wasn't a man anywhere unless he was a really old, old person. And about that time, those airplanes flew over. They were going to bomb the miners.' You never saw an airplane in 1921, right? Dad said that everyone just looked up like this, spellbound, standing just like frozen there, looking at those planes. Then all once one of the women said, 'They're going to bomb us!' just like that, and panic struck everyone. Dad said my grandmother grabbed him under one arm and my uncle Arnold under another –my Uncle Arnold would have been about three then –started running, and ran into a tent, shoved them under the bed, crawled under the bed with them until the airplanes were gone. And the history is that they did drop bombs, but not on these family members. They dropped them on the miners, trying to get to Blair Mountain. The pilots were throwing bombs over the side of the planes. And the woman who screamed out, 'They're going to bomb us,' was right. She just didn't know who. And Dad told us the story so eloquently, as though it happened the day before. My Dad never lost one bit of mental faculties until he died. And same with my mother. She is 92. Sharp as a tack. Both of them. I've been very much blessed with respect to that."

## COUSIN MURDERED

**Roberts:** "My Dad told another story. This was when he was five years old, too. They were living in Seng Creek at that time. I don't know if you know where Seng Creek is. From Kayford, you go through what used to be the tunnel. On the other side of the tunnel, that's called Seng Creek as you went down off the mountain on that road leading into Whitesville on the Boone County side. They were living there. And my grandfather's cousin and one of the Baldwin-Felts' guards started having trouble and obviously did not like each other at all."

**Kline:** Baldwin-Felts?

**Roberts:** "Yeah, guards. Some people called them thugs but they were out of (a security agency) in Bluefield. You know, they were notorious. They were around for most of the strikes in West Virginia, but starting back in 1912, 1913 on Paint Creek and Cabin Creek, they were pretty much agents of the company, similar to some of the former detective agencies that were formed to break strikes in other industries. If you saw the movie *Matewan,* those were Baldwin-Felts guards that

Sid Hatfield killed in the streets there. So you had these guards to do the company's bidding. Grandfather was very much Union and I guess his relatives were all Union too. But my grandfather's cousin was having trouble back and forth with this Baldwin-Felts guard. And they had a large, two-story building there. Downstairs was a bar. Upstairs was an old silent movie theater. To get to the theater you walked up the steps on the side of the building. The Baldwin-Felts guard —this was the middle of day— was at the bar drinking. And he saw my grandfather's cousin walking up those steps. He went outside and killed him, and as he walked up the steps shot him about five times. And our cousin rolled down the steps.

   "In those days, they didn't have funeral homes. So what did you do with someone that's dead? Well, they brought this body to my grandfather's house. My Dad was five in those days, right? And they took the door off the hinges and took a chair, put it here and a chair there, and laid the door across the chairs to make a slab, and picked the body up and laid it on the door. Then they took all of the clothes off of my grandfather's cousin. A doctor came and plugged the bullet holes up with cotton where he'd been shot so he wouldn't bleed anymore. See you didn't have a mortuary, anything like that. And then they went over to the boarding house where he lived and got his suit. All the miners had one good suit in those days, I guess. If you can imagine a five year old watching this, they put the suit on him. And then they went to the carpenter shop at the company and got a pine box. That's who made the coffins in those days. They brought the pine box over. Then they took the body off the door and put it down in the coffin, nailed it shut right there in the living room, took him to the railroad station and shipped his body back to Kentucky where he was from. And then put the door back on its hinges. Dad told that story just like he saw it yesterday morning. He had the best memory, best storyteller you ever heard and he never missed a beat telling that story. So, I heard lots and lots of stories about the Union and coal mining growing up."

## KIN TO THE BLIZZARDS

**Kline:** Somebody told me that you are somehow related to the Blizzards?

**Roberts:** "Oh, yeah. Oh, yes."

**Kline:** I've always wondered about Ma Blizzard.

**Roberts:** "Ma Blizzard raised my mother. I've tried to figure out exactly what age my Mom started living with Ma Blizzard. She must have been around 10 or 11. And she lived with Ma Blizzard until she got married. When Dad and she got married, they didn't want to tell Ma Blizzard. How's that going to work? My Mom told me the story that Dad was frightened to tell Ma. But they eventually did. My mother worked in Ma Blizzard's restaurant for years and years."

**Kline:** And that was where?

**Roberts:** "Eskdale. Eskdale was a very significant place because when miners went on strike on Cabin Creek in 1912 and 1913, everything on Cabin Creek was owned by the coal company, except Eskdale. They used to joke and say that their town was the 'free state' of Eskdale. And Ma Blizzard gave the striking miners (evicted from the company houses) property to put their tents on. That's how she got the name of Mother Blizzard by the miners.

They thought of her the same as they thought of Mother Jones. Mother Jones used to stay at Mother Blizzard's home. A lot of people didn't know that. My grandmother Harlow recalled that when she was a little girl, Mother Jones came to stay with Mother Blizzard. When she was older, she used to tell me about meeting Mother Jones at Mother Blizzard's. So my family, yeah, they were very proud the fact that they built the union in West Virginia. They also you know, historically knew that Mother Jones and others who were very famous in the annals of labor history.

"Bill Blizzard (who led the march on Blair Mountain in August of 1921) was Mother Blizzard's son. He would be my great-uncle. And he was my Grandmother Harlow's brother. And I never really met him because at that time I was, you know, a teenager. Even before that his career was over and finished with the Union. But I heard a lot about him from people talking. My mother used to say a lot of the Union officials came into the restaurant on Cabin Creek, from District 17 and other places. So she got to meet a lot of those people in her lifetime. They called it Ma Blizzard's Restaurant. Oh I remember that restaurant —."

**Kline:** Was there a counter to sit at or tables? What did she serve?

**Roberts:** "Oh, hot dogs, hamburgers and barbeques pretty much. And I guess they had pies and stuff like that. But she told me she served many a coal miner, many a Union official, sandwiches.

"My mother told me this story. People could sell beer, you know. And Bill Blizzard thought that Ma

Blizzard ought to get a beer license, start selling beer because there's lots of money to be made. Believe it or not, coal miners like to drink beer occasionally, not to mention everybody else on Cabin Creek. But Frank Blizzard —Frank Blizzard was Bill's brother — eventually took over Ma Blizzard's restaurant and turned it into a beer tavern. One end of it, ironically, sold ice cream and hotdogs. And they had curb service. The other end became pretty much a beer joint after Mother Blizzard gave it up. So Frank took it over and he sold beer for many, many years there. And they still sold sandwiches. But they had an ice cream-like custard stand attached to the other end, so people could pull in and get curb service or walk in and get ice cream, or go inside and drink beer. Lots and lots of folks came to the place. It was like 'the place to go' on Cabin Creek in those days, I guess. But when Mother Blizzard had it, for the most part it was a restaurant."

## IMMIGRANTS AND STRIKES ON CABIN CREEK

**Roberts:** "In 1912 there were 6,000 people on strike on Cabin Creek. Mother Jones spoke at the Cabin Creek junction. They said that there were 6,000 people in attendance. So, coal mining was very labor intensive in those days. And thousands and thousand of people were working in those coal mines."

**Kline:** And you probably heard about every kind of language spoken, didn't you?

**Roberts:** "If you go back and read the history of the United Mine Workers, it was formed by immigrants when they had the first convention in Columbus, Ohio, in 1890 on January 25th. That is amazing that they were able to organize it because they really couldn't speak to teach other. The [United Mine Workers] Journal used to be printed, I think, in 20-some different languages. You know, I've heard people came from all over the world to mine coal in places like West Virginia and eastern Kentucky. So when they had the first convention, I guess they had to have somebody try to interpret for them. And the union they formed is still around. That's just an amazing story. I think the movie *Matewan* does a great job of depicting what it was like to be on strike with people from different countries and different cultures trying to understand each other and still stand up against the companies."

## SHOPPING AT KROGERS

**Roberts:** "Dad told another story about how he and Mom had the audacity one time to go to Krogers and shop. Krogers is a big food chain everyone in West Virginia is familiar with. Later he reports to work and the superintendent comes out and asks him if he's been shopping somewhere besides the company store. And Dad acknowledged that they had. And the superintendent said, 'I want to tell you something, we have just as good products at our company stores as they do anywhere else and we expect our employees to shop at the company store'. And that day they gave Daddy a bad place to load coal. In those days, you were hand-loading the coal. They would send you wherever they wanted you to load coal. Well, they sent him to work in a place that had water standing in it as a punishment for shopping at Krogers. So there were ways to force you to deal with the company store. We always did deal at the company store when I was growing up. We used to go to the Kayford Company Store, Acme Company Store, Leewood Company Store, Rhonda Company Store. When I started work in the mines, I bought my first pair of boots, my hard hat and belt at the Winifred Company Store—it was owned by Carbon Fuel—because it was hard to find hard hats and a belt and boots anywhere else. So, the company stores were around when I started mining coal in the 1970s."

## FIRST DAY IN THE HOLE

**Kline:** Tell us, you must have some memories of your first day in the mines, do you?

**Roberts:** (Laughing) "Yes. (Laughing) I think I was 23. I'd been in the Army, been to Vietnam. And then went to work in the mines. The first day was a Friday, I remember very well. Scared to death, terrified. Although my Dad had been a miner all his life, I was nervous as I could be. Started on the day shift. And in those days someone had to sign a paper to be responsible for you. A miner named Joe Pratt who was in his 50's, signed for me that day. I still remember it very well. The man-trip [a conveyance that transported workers to the coal face] was outside on the tracks. Didn't have a cover over it because the mine was too low for a canopy. The average height in that mine was 42 inches but, it got down to as low as 36 inches in some places. And when you laid down on the top of the cars that made up the mantrip, you had to lay on your side. And if you raised up, you could touch the top of the coal seam as you rolled underground from the drift mouth. And Joe Pratt says to me, 'Son, don't raise up. If you raise up you'll get your head tore off.' That was the first instruction he gave me. Said, 'Don't raise up, you'll get your head tore off.' So as we rode under ground, I'm lying on my side and I can see the top right above me. I'm looking around this mine and I'm thinking,

'Oh my goodness!' And the further we went underground, the more nervous I got.

"We get to where our section is, and all these older guys jump off the man-trip and they just take off walking. But you can't stand up. I can't figure out how to walk. They were walking all bent over like this and just flying up the section. I'm hitting my head and I'm falling down. It was a chore just to get up on the section. And then they gave me a shovel and I shoveled all day, cleaning the ribs. You can't have loose coal in the ribs, right? You've got to clean that up and put it in the middle of the walkways so that the loading machine can pick it up. And I'm doing that and I'm thinking after while, 'It's got to be lunchtime,' you know. 'They've forgot about me,' is just what I'm thinking, and then more time goes by. And then gosh, 'It's got to be three o'clock. They forgot about me all together here.' And then after what I thought was three o'clock passed, they came to me and told me it was eleven o'clock. And it seemed like an eternity. They let me go eat. When I went back to work from eating, I was loading or shoveling coal again. By the time I got back outside, I was exhausted. And we didn't work on Saturdays in those days. Some people did. They posted notice of who they wanted to work. Saturday, I could hardly get out of bed. I was trying to walk, hurt from the top of my head to the tip of my toes. And then on Monday I had to go back and try it again. And I'm thinking, 'I wonder if I can do this?' But I made myself to go back. After about a month of this, you finally get used to it. You learn how to walk, you lean how to get around in the mines. Things become more familiar to you, but it took a while. It was hard. But I stuck it out. I had a wife and two kids to take care of. So it was interesting to say the least. It was hard.

"But after while, I think coal miners don't look at their jobs any different than someone going to work in an auto factory or for that matter, going to work in a studio. I was on *Crossfire* one time on CNN. And one of the panelists said to me, 'So people here' —he was talking about Washington— 'can't understand why anybody wants to work in the mines.' I said, 'Well people where I came from can't understand why anybody wants to live in Washington. So there you go.' (Laughs) So, they said, 'You've got a good point.' But coal miners, once they got used to mining coal, that's the workplace. And after a while you don't think about it any differently than anybody else going to work might think about their workplace. We know we are working in a dangerous place. We know we have to look after our safety and look after each other. But it's not like we get up everyday dreading to go to work or hating to go to work. It's our job, right? And we take a lot of pride in it.

## A FAVORITE PHOTO: THE PITTSTON STRIKE

**Kline:** When we came in, out in the hallway we saw a picture of you, exchanging pleasantries with a—

**Roberts:** (laughing)

**Kline:** State Police man? Tell us about that.

**Roberts:** "That is one of my favorite pictures, perhaps ever. That was during the Pittston strike when we had taken over and occupied the Moss Three Preparation Plant. We had 99 of our members and one minister go into the preparation plant on a Sunday afternoon—caught them off guard. I say caught them off guard, that would have been the company, their security team, which was an advanced security team, and the State Police. The State

Police, we determined, switched out [changed their shifts] about that time on Sundays. The ones finishing up their shift were leaving and others were arriving to work at about that time. So they weren't prepared. And we rushed in, took over the preparation plant. And then we had —"

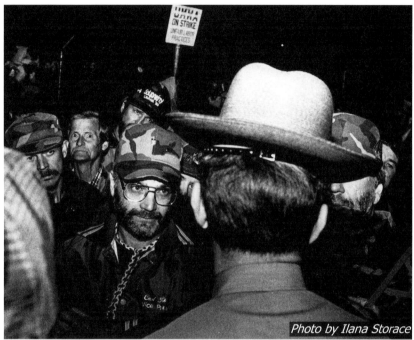

Photo by Ilana Storace

Cecil Roberts (with glasses) leads fellow strikers at Moss Three Pittston mine in September of 1998.

**Kline:** 99?

**Roberts:** "Ninety-nine strikers and one minister—but we had 1200, 1400 strikers outside—rushed in by car caravan about same moment. We held that plant from Sunday afternoon until Wednesday night. And no one could come in or go out without our permission. And the police, the U.S. Marshals, judges, federal and state, none of them could do anything about it. They fined us very heavily, obviously. But that was a significant victory for the Union and it sent a loud clear message to the company that we were not going away. So about the second day there, the U.S. Marshals came out to serve us an injunction ordering us out of there. The State Police were gathered around also. So in that picture you see the state police, but there were also U.S. Marshals there with guns on. And we're into a conversation with them about how they were going to serve all one hundred people that were in the plant, as well as ourselves and John Cox who was with me, and others. By the time that ended on Wednesday—we always had rallies on Wednesday nights in St Pau—since we were at the preparation plant, we just had a rally there. And the Roanoke Times ran a story and they estimated a crowd of about 5,000 outside that plant on Wednesday night. They said it was like 'a Billy Graham crusade at altar call time' is how they described it. There was music and speeches. We had the miners from inside the plant come out and drop their backpacks and everything in a truck. And got them out of there while we had a big crowd on hand so the police could not identify them and arrest them. It was probably a highlight of my career during the Moss Three takeover in the Pittston strike of September, 1989."

## THE WEST VIRGINIA STATE MUSEUM

**Kline:** Well now, I'll tell you. I got my first look at the Coal Exhibit at the State Museum at the Culture Center in Charleston last week. And I went there having seen your letter of July 26, in which you laid out some concerns you had about the exhibit. And having recently seen the exhibit I can't find that it reflects the details you've been telling me over the last forty minutes about your own life in the coal fields. The story just isn't there. It doesn't come alive. You would think the people who developed that exhibit, that none of them had ever seen a coal mine or even talked to a coal miner. None of this you're telling me is reflected in that exhibit. And I'm wondering how you feel about it.

**Roberts:** "I think, as I looked at the museum, maybe I'm wrong, but it seemed to me that they were trying to speak to how they would like to see our history perceived, as opposed to how our history is. (Laughs) What I mean by that is, I think the State —and I understand their perspective on this— wanted to project to the rest of the country a better image of the coal industry in West Virginia. So they worked from that perspective, as opposed to working from a perspective of let's tell the actual, factual history of coal mining and the Union and the struggles and trials and tribulations that existed throughout the years."

"Two things I think that jump out at you. First, the exhibit's assertion of how great the coal company stores were, that they were really the forerunners of the credit card. I mean, that is the most absurd description imaginable with respect to what the company stores were. You are really stretching things a mile to say that the company stores were the forerunners of credit cards and how wonderful that was. I don't think there are very many people who would say, 'I wish the company stores would come back, I wish I can go back to that company store again and pay more [than other local stores charged]. I wish I was obligated to go back to the company store.' You just never hear anyone say that.

"Another [detail of the exhibit] that was totally misleading, I thought, and inappropriate, is the way they describe the Monongah explosion. That was the worst industrial accident in the history of our country, period. The official number of miners killed there is listed as 362, but the real number is probably closer to 500 people, because in those days, you could take someone with you, maybe your brother or your son, whatever—and they were contract miners [and not officially counted]—to go in and help you load coal. So the truth is, I don't think anyone knows the actual number killed. It is probably closer to 500 than 362. For whatever reason, some museum designer felt it necessary to say how wonderful Christmas was that year because the company gave the grieving families bonuses. There is no way that could have been a wonderful Christmas. What is the point of saying that? I mean, this is the greatest tragedy in our industrial history. But we think we have an obligation somehow to say that it was not a bad Christmas? It was a terrible Christmas! It would be a horrendous Christmas for everybody who lost a father or son or brother or friend. I thought it was just totally, completely self-serving, a real slap in the face to all those miners who died there and their families, and friends. I mean, if you read the account that McAteer wrote about in his book, the most recent accounting of the tragedy there: In the weeks following the explosion at Monongah, three other major mine disasters occurred, prompting the last month of 1907 to be nicknamed "Black December." In the final tally, 3,241 American miners were killed on the job that year, the largest number killed in a single year in this country's history. In spite of such horrific accidents, many mining operations, including Monongah, continued to ignore recognized safety precautions, using open candles instead of shielded lamps, employing cheap dynamite instead of controllable explosives, and skipping tests that would detect methane gas. Such practices were already being followed in Europe.

**Roberts:**    "Almost of all those miners were immigrants. And some of them hadn't brought their families to West Virginia or the United States yet. So it was even tough trying to figure out who to notify. It was just a horrendous and terrible time in West Virginia. I mean, why can't we just say that this was a terrible tragedy. It was painful and it was hurtful and leave it at that, because that's the truth. And for someone to say, 'Let's think of something good say about the company here.' (Laughing) Why, you don't have to do that. If something happened, say it and move on.

"I'm proud of our industry now for trying to make mines safer and I think 95% of the companies are trying to do what's right by improving safety. But you got 5% out there that the federal government and the state government just have to make do what's right. They just have to do that. That's why we have laws. It keeps good companies continuing to be good companies and bad companies, making them do what's right. And that's just the way it is. I don't think you take history and say, 'Well, what can we say good about the other side here?' That's not really history, is it? When you have this tragedy, what's the point of talking about the bonuses that somebody got? Goodness gracious. It was not certainly a good Christmas, right?"

**Kline:** It couldn't have been.

**Roberts:** "Yeah."

**Kline:** So what do you think that the museum's going to do, or what would you like to see the museum do about all of this?

**Roberts:** "To me a museum tells me a story and it tells the truth. Whatever the truth is that's what they should tell. I don't think there's very many people who would say, 'I wish the company stores would come back, I wish I owed my soul to the company store.' Who can you hear saying that? No one. If the company stores were that great they'd still be here, wouldn't they? They are not here anymore and there is a reason for that: because they weren't a good thing. They might have been a necessary thing in some instances. But it doesn't mean that they were good thing. Let's just tell the truth about company stores, right? Let's tell the truth about the tragedies we've had and just leave it at that."

## SUGAR COATING THE TRUTH

**Roberts:** "Someone when they put this museum together said, 'We have an obligation here to figure out something good to say about both sides.' I don't really know, in the case of museums, if you have sides. It's just a history of your state, right? You don't have an obligation to say something good about the coal companies if you say something bad about the coal companies. We should be proud of the industry we have now just trying to do better and provide jobs. That doesn't mean that a hundred years ago it was like that, or 50 years ago it was like that. The truth is we had to bring the government kicking and screaming to the aid of the coal miners. The government didn't come and drag the coal miners kicking and screaming to have better laws. The coal miners had to give up theirs lives, had to strike and fight and everything else to get the government to be on their side. That's the truth. That is as true as it can be. And you can't sugarcoat that, you can't change that. That's a fact. Museums are supposed to be about facts and history and what happened, not what you would've liked to have happen, see happen, not what you wish had happened. But is that exhibit telling the truth when 100 other people are saying, 'That is not way it was.'? So I think museums are historical presentations that should be factual."

**Kline:** And do you feel that that should be their obligation?

**Roberts:** "I don't think there is any doubt that it should be their obligation. If you're going to have a museum —. If it is not a museum that's presenting facts, call it something else. 'This is the way we wish it was.' (Laughing) How about that? (Laughing) I don't know what you call that. It's some kind of presentation, but it's not a factual one."

**Kline:** Do you hold out any hope that they are going to straighten that up?

**Roberts:** "I always hold out hope for everything, but it doesn't mean that it's going to happen. I don't know why this museum was put together in the manner that it was. They claimed that they had all these historians that verified what they placed in the museum. I would like to have an opportunity to meet these historians, and maybe sit around a table like this and let's talk about it."

**Kline:** With these historians?

**Roberts:** "Yes, whoever they are. Where did they get —. What books, what kinds of authority did they have? I mean, are they experts in this field? Are they really historians? Where did they get their information? What did they rely on to come to these kinds of conclusions? Who did they talk to? Out of hundreds and thousands of, perhaps a million people who lived through this, what percentage of those people did they talk to who gave them this kind of description of the way life was in those days, which is obviously [in the case of the 'Coal' exhibit at the Cultural Center] very contrary to what most of people remember?

"I think it's really important for tourists to see [authentic exhibits] and come away saying good things about West Virginia. There are a lot of good things to say about West Virginia. But you can't make the Civil War sound like something nice, can you? You can't take the Civil Rights movement and sugar coat it and say it was all just peachy keen and fine and dandy. Bull Conners was Bull Conners, right? You can work all day long and you can't make him a good person. And you can't make people who murdered Civil Rights leaders good people, can you? You can't make company stores good things either. It might have been convenient, it might have been necessary in a lot of instances, but you can't say these were wonderful things for coal miners. It just wasn't that way. Many miners were head-over-heels in debt to them. And the truth is that if the miners had had more flexibility, more freedom to shop, they could have gotten by more economically than they did shopping at the company stories. But even that is not the thing that really stands out to me. It's the characterization of the Monongah disaster and trying to make Christmas seem like a good time or applaud companies if they did give money to families. I'm sure they did but that doesn't make this thing go away or make it any better."

## ARDENT SOCIALIST?

**Kline:** What about referring to Bill Blizzard and other leaders of the March in 1921 as ardent socialists?

**Roberts:** (Laughing) "First of all, how did they know what Bill Blizzard's views were? I think, I've actually heard that Bill Blizzard might have been a Republican. (Laughs) I don't know if that's the same as a Socialist or not. It might be (Laughs). I don't know what Bill Blizzard's politics were. But let's be fair here. Anyone that's ever stood up for workers in the history of this country has been called something, and 'a Socialist' is one of the things that people might lay on you, or worse, if you are fighting for folks. Some people believe that you should just support the capitalistic system and the people in power. That's why one percent of our country is doing fine. And 99% of us aren't. If 99% of us would like to see things better, what does that make us? The One Percent thinks we're socialists, right?"

**Kline:** I'm sure.

**Roberts:** "I'm sure they do. And I'm sure they call us names from time to time. But I think we are just trying to get our fair share of what the capitalistic system produces. And I don't think it is fair to call Bill Blizzard anything in particular. But you have to look at the times too. I think Frank Keeney openly acknowledged that he was a Socialist, but back in those days it wasn't that uncommon, right? I mean he was standing up for workers. Eugene Debs ran for the presidency several times and got millions of votes, right?

"What they are trying to do [in the 'Coal' exhibit] is to use today's definition of what someone might perceive of as a 'Socialist,' or left-leaning person, and apply it to make this [historic figure] seem like a radical and out of touch. But in those days, both Keeney and Bill Blizzard were very popular people, regardless of their politics."

**Kline:** Well, the exhibit nowhere refers to the coal operators as "rabid capitalists," either.

**Roberts:** "You might have applied something even worse than that to them."

**Kline:** Sure.

**Roberts:** "But there is no historical benefit in name calling either to coal operators or, for that matter, to leaders of the Union. I think what we should do is to state facts about how workers were exploited. I don't recall reading anywhere in that museum that workers were exploited. Now, does that make it untrue? It's absolutely true that workers were exploited. Workers who were being paid by the ton back in 1912 and 1913 and all through the 1920s had a company checkweighman (to tally the car load), and you had to load 2500 or 3000 pounds to get credit for a 'company ton.' The company check weigh man lied about how much you mined. On payday days, if you don't get any money, what are you? But by the time they deducted for the company store, the company house, and the company doctor, and the company tools you used, you got zero. You worked 16 hours a day loading coal and if you didn't get paid, what does it make you? It makes you what? A slave! I'm reminded that as late as 1985, Don Blankenship made a speech in Huntington and he said, 'If everyone would work for nothing, everyone would have a job.' That is absolutely true. But that makes you what? A slave, which is the same thing that you had in 1912, 1913, up through 1920s."

## WEEKENDS AND VACATIONS

**Roberts:** "This situation existed until the Wagner Act was passed in the mid '30s giving people legal right to join the Union. What happened when they had the legal right? Why did hundreds, millions of people, for that matter, rush to join unions when the Wager Act passed? Because they wanted to have a better way of life. And when did the middle class come of age? It was when workers had the right to join unions. And then they could get paid a fair day's pay for a fair day's work. They could have vacations, and they could have pensions, they could have healthcare, they could actually send their kids off to school.

"And people today badmouth the unions like they were the worst thing in the world. A lot of those people ought to go back and look at how they got those benefits: because some unions or a group of unions fought for those things. Until we had the legal right in this country to join unions, we had none of those things. That's when things got better in the coal fields. That's when things got better in the auto industry, steel industry. That's when things got better across this country and the middle class was born. So, I always say when you see a union person, thank them for the vacation you are going on, or the healthcare and wages you have, or personal leave days, floating vacation days, or whatever you have."

**Kline:** Like the weekend?

**Roberts:** "Week-ends, yeah, brought you by organized labor, right?" (Laughs)

**Kline:** Wow. This has been great.

**Roberts:** "Oh, good."

**Kline:** "Is there anything else that you'd like to talk about, or that I should ask you?"

**Roberts:** "I just think we owe so much to those people who went before us. Up until the passage of the Wagner Act, working class people were not in the middle class. Coal miners were still struggling. When the Wagner Act was passed, millions of people joined unions. And people went on marches and sit down strikes in the auto industry, and strikes in the coal industry. Then we had Lewis who fought for the 1946-47 Health and Retirement Act, health and retirement provisions of the contract and brought us all into the middle class, starting in 1935 and moving up into the '50s. And for many years in this country, if you contributed to the production of the auto industry, or contributed to the production of coal, you got your fair share of what had been produced. As you look around now, the top one percent is getting the most of it. And there is not much left for the rest of us. That's what's wrong with the country now. We need, I think, more power in organized labor to give the people a stronger, more powerful voice in order to get a greater share of the wealth they are producing so that all of us can enjoy the benefits of middle class (living), not just that a tiny fraction of our society."

**Kline:** You have spoken now twice about being introverted as a younger man —

**Roberts:** (Laughing) "Yeah."

**Kline:** I wonder if you can remember the moment when you —. Or was there a particular situation when you found your voice?

**Roberts:** "I think it started in the Army, and then, I think, continued on and probably developed to a great extent when I became a local Union officer and spokesperson for that small group of people I was representing. Ours was a pretty radical local, and you had to learn to speak up for what you believed and defend yourself in arguments. And then I was given an opportunity to come out of the mines for a couple of weeks. I received training from the Federal Mediation and Conciliation Service and was given an opportunity to teach classes for four months. That's where I think things really took off for me, to stand in front of other miners day in and day out, teaching classes on labor history, how to file grievances, past practices and customs, all these things that help people become better local union representatives. The Union had me doing that for four months back in 1976. And that's probably what opened every door to me for moving up in the Union, which I think really blossomed into where I am now."

**Kline:** So, is your experience a reflection of the mission in the United Mine Workers to provide rank and file education?

**Roberts:** "Yes, this was something Arnold Miller envisioned in District 17, being his home district, and actually paid for this. I think Arnold had a lot of great ideas, quite frankly. And I think his health probably prevented him from reaching the pinnacle he would like to have achieved. Arnold actually envisioned having a continuing education department at the UMWA to educate miners and particularly leaders, an ongoing, never ending educational process growing out of an educational department at the Union. And if we could do that now, it would be something great. We do a lot of education but we don't have what I would call an educational department here. Miller had that vision, and I think it is correct one, all the way back in the '70s. We still do education for our safety committee men because we have a heavy emphasis here on protecting workers. But the earlier plan in the '70s would have expanded from that, to teach labor history and contract education, how to present cases and win cases, what you need to be good witnesses, things of that nature. I loved the labor history part of it, myself. That's when I started trying to learn as much as I could about our history so that I could teach it to others. Arnold Miller had a lot of great ideas. Unfortunately his health didn't allow him to act on all of them."

**Kline:** Thank you very much.

**Roberts:** "Thank you. I enjoyed it."

# Hidden Coffins Unearth Needed History
Fr. John S. Rausch

Fr. John Rausch, a Glenmary priest, is the Director of the Catholic Committee of Appalachia. He was recipient of the 2007 "Teacher of Peace" award presented by Pax, Christi, U.S.A.

At the intersection of Rt. 612 and Scarbro Road, just outside Oak Hill, West Virginia, the Whipple Colliery Company Store stands as a two-story structure with a massive flight of steps that leads a visitor into the central merchandising room of the store's commissary. Just off from the spacious room a hand-operated freight elevator connects the basement storage area of this late nineteenth century building with the main floor and the top floor frequently festooned for the owner's ballroom dances.

Curiously, a secret space is sandwiched between these first and second floors. This hidden area, just five feet high and accessible only by elevator, housed the coffins the company deemed necessary as a cost of digging coal. Keeping the coffins out of sight reduced the stress on both wives and miners who shopped at the store, but they played an integral role in coal mining and were needed almost every day.

"The coffins would service three mines in the area," says Joy Lynn, co-owner and curator of the Whipple Company Store Museum and Learning Center. "Some days they'd need forty, some days they'd need ten, some days one and some days sixty. We're talking about the period between 1893 and 1930."

## Learning History, Seeing a Vision

Unfortunately today, few Americans grasp the significance of the sufferings our forebearers endured to create the working conditions that insure a more dignified workplace. Child labor laws, the eight hour workday, workman's compensation, Social Security and retirement programs, health and safety laws—all taken for granted today—represent progressive reforms supported by organized labor, the church, and people of faith.

The point: people of faith especially need to learn where the coffins of history are kept! Unlike the Ten Commandments that were given by God and inscribed in the heart of every believer, the social teachings of the Catholic church came from reflections about earning a living in a capitalist system. For more than a century the church observed the conditions of workers, the abuse of immigrants and the power of capital to manipulate creation and communities. From those observations it established social principles for engaging in commercial life while treating workers with fairness and justice. While not strictly based on class analysis, these theological reflections proclaim a fundamental option for the poor and strive to balance the rights of individuals with their call to community. Not as a rugged individual nor as someone lost in an amorphous collective, the church sees each worker as a person-in-community who shares dignity and vision with co-workers who are brothers and sisters.

As globalization, new technologies and a greater awareness of environmental concerns change the nature of work, the church's social principles continue to challenge individual workers and structures to ask what the economic system is doing for people, what is it doing to people and how people are participating. Without a sense of history and an awareness of the present, no realistic vision will inspire the future. And, without a vision, the people will perish. In a sense, people of faith today wonder where the coffins are kept.

## Early Working Conditions

With the flowering of the Industrial Revolution in the latter part of the nineteenth century the demand for coal grew exponentially to fuel the steel mills and electrical generating plants dotting the countryside. Frequently, safety concerns took a backseat to the demands for production.

In 1869 the Avondale Colliery located in Luzerne County, Pensylvania, suffered the largest human loss to that date with 110 miners killed when the wooden breaker constructed over the only exit shaft caught fire, trapping and suffocating the workers below. That era saw miners die daily from rock falls, premature blasts, or railway car accidents.

The deadliest year for American mining, 1907, witnessed the deaths of 3,242 workers with hundreds at a time losing their lives. Monongah, West Virginia, became the worst mining disaster in U.S. history when a blast caused by the ignition of methane gas and coal dust killed 362 workers officially, but because family members— frequently sons and even wives—customarily dug coal with the miners to make their minimal wage, historians think the number could have exceeded 500 fatalities. Just two weeks later at Darr, Pennsylvania, another 239 workers, mainly Hungarian immigrants, perished from a similar cause. During this era mining companies proved callous and cavalier about human safety, striving instead to protect the expensive mine mules and ponies at the expense of their cheap and abundant immigrant labor force. The twentieth century alone saw over 100,000 coal miners killed in U.S. mines with an untold larger number suffocating from black lung or "miner's asthma."

Working conditions in most industries put profits before people and set workers, with few rights, against bosses with little mercy. The storied Triangle Shirtwaist Company fire as one of America's worst industrial accidents demonstrates the disregard for workers. In 1911, on a Saturday afternoon when workers began thinking about their Sunday off, a fire started on the eighth floor of the ten-story Asch Building in Manhattan where the Triangle Company occupied the top three floors with 500 workers. The flames spread quickly to the upper floors trapping many amid the burning fabric and trimmings that lay bundled and loose in numerous piles. Witnesses reported the horror of seeing workers, many embracing one another, leap to their deaths from windows as the fire engulfed them. The tragic toll numbered 146 dead, mostly immigrant girls and women, with scores more seriously injured, because the two freight elevators failed as an escape after the owners locked the stairwell doors.

More than a century ago workers regularly logged twelve hour shifts six days a week. In 1880 one sixth of American workers (1,118,000) were children under the age of sixteen. In 1889 alone 22,000 railroad workers were killed or injured on the job. Because wages fluctuated with the economy, the Carnegie Steel Company in 1892 cut pay between 18% and 26% leading to the Homestead Strike that ended in bloody violence. A little more than a century ago the human dignity of American workers was sacrificed to a new wave of industrialization.

## The Dignity and Rights of Workers

This history represented the type of conditions that prompted people of faith to speak out about human dignity and the rights of workers. Pope Leo XIII wrote his groundbreaking encyclical, Rerum Novarum, in 1891 that rejected both an unbridled capitalism that could deny workers their God-given human dignity, and an ultra powerful state that could destroy their self-determined human initiative. In that seminal document the Catholic Church clearly promoted unions, a just wage and the renewal of the social order.

For people of faith, however, the dignity of workers rests not on any privilege afforded by the state, or any argument offered from economic theory, but on moral and ethical laws that originate from the nature of the human person. Each worker is made in the image and likeness of God and we are all our brother's (and sister's) keeper. This theological statement forms the basis for the dignity of each worker and the worker's call to community and the common good.

To protect their dignity and to recognize all people as social beings, workers have a right to form a union. Because the employer has so much power, unions act as a countervailing force to level the playing field so workers can demand safe and decent working conditions. They also need a just wage to maintain their families, health care to insure their strength, and retirement benefits to guarantee a dignified old age. Because workers are not machines, they need periods of rest, not only to rejuvenate their bodies for more work, but to become fully integrated persons, i.e. people who can appreciate beauty and the arts, and grow spiritually.

With this view of human dignity, the notion of work becomes something beyond simply earning a livelihood. Work participates in divine activity. God worked. God rested on the seventh day after God worked to create the heavens and the earth. Then God invited humanity into the labor force by placing humanity (Adam) in the garden "to care and cultivate it" (Gen. 2:15). So humanity becomes a co-gardener with God! Yes, people work to earn a livelihood, but they also work for self-fulfillment, to feel good about themselves, and ultimately to contribute to society and make a difference.

A celebrated parable describes a reporter interviewing three workers at a building site. Asked what he was doing, the first responded, "I'm laying bricks." The second ventured a further description: "I'm building a wall." But the third worker shared his experience with enthusiasm and glee: "Can't you see, I'm building a cathedral!" Same activity, same work, different vision.

## Begin With Solidarity

Workers need a way to build "their cathedrals" at work, and unions offer the best structure for workers' rights. Yet, one myth with wide currency says that unions, once needed in the past to counter unregulated capitalism, are now passé because of today's environmental and labor laws.

In July, 2002, nine coal miners working the Quecreek Mine near Somerset, Pennsylvania, punched through a wall to an abandoned mine and felt the fury of 150 million gallons of water gushing through the breach. Scrambling for their lives the miners ran in crouched position through a four and a half foot high passage seeking higher ground as the rising water engulfed them. With the water to their necks, then their chins, the men pulled themselves along the main conveyor belt and finally found an 18 foot by 30 foot patch of high ground where they rested and waited for help.

On the Pennsylvania hillside the drama took place on two stages–above with the rescue workers and below among the trapped miners. Topside, the rescue team used global satellite positioning equipment—with a dash of common sense—to target the air pocket. The most advanced technology and the sharpest engineering minds worked to free the miners.

Below, the men lived "nine for nine"–everyone would survive, or the team would die together. Drenched from fighting the water, they sat back-to-back to preserve body heat. Two men sandwiched a third shaking from hypothermia. They encouraged one another and kept their spirits high. Through their belts they looped plastic coated cable and tied themselves together.

Finally, after 78 hours, cheers erupted when the men emerged one by one from the escape cage to the glare of cameras and the embrace of rescuers.

On balance, technology contributed its part to the rescue, but the miners' spirit proved essential. Tethered to one another "nine for nine," the miners offered the world an important metaphor by demonstrating their code of solidarity.

Yet, at a hearing about the Quecreek accident some months later, Jeffrey Mihallik, a Safety Committeeman from the United Mine Workers of America, said the accident should never have happened and reminded the panel that under any UMWA contract union members can refuse to work in unsafe conditions. Non-union miners, like those at Quecreek, do not enjoy such protection. They either go in, or go home.

## Discover the New Vision

Unions continue to play their traditional role safeguarding the rights of workers with contracts and political representation. Local union safety committees make union mines safer than non-union mines by creating a "safety effect," thus lowering the serious injury and fatality rate. And, unions not only secure higher wages for their own members, but through the "threat effect" force non-union mines to pay comparable wages to keep the union out. Also, the social milestones like child labor laws, Social Security and the eight-hour day have fingerprints from the union movement all over them.

Yet, today unions with churches and progressive institutions face the challenge of revising the self-image of workers and the middle class from rugged individualists to people of community. At the turn of the 20th century industrial barons endeavored to split the working class by convincing people their self-interest lay in becoming consumers, thus weakening their allegiance to progressive groups. The emphasis began the long gradual shift to concern for individual gain without regard for the environment, the local community or the common good.

Social commentator Msgr. George Higgins (1916 -2002), known as the "labor priest," wrote: "American workers need a raise, but they need more than a raise. They need a vision–a vision of economic citizenship."

That economic citizenship means involvement in life beyond shopping. It entails a voice in the workplace, volunteering in the local community and speaking out for a healthy environment. While social legislation wove a safety net intended for all, the fact remains that legislation gave it, and legislation can take it away. Without due vigilance the strands of labor's safety net can fray, or be cut, for short term profits and the company's stock value.

Economic citizenship means shopping with regard for the dignity of the worker overseas, and buying in solidarity with the worker in the local community. The "cheapest price" consideration must be balanced with the "social implication" of the purchase. And, with only one planet to sustain life, economic citizenship means practicing a stewardship of creation.

## The Journey

How many strikes and marches, how many speeches and sermons, how many pieces of legislation it took during the history of labor to secure the minimal rights of workers! Labor historians can appreciate Avondale, Monongah and Darr contributing to the vision that workers deserve a safe environment and a place of respect and dignity. People of faith can deepen that conviction with moral and ethical principles, but they must first reflect on where the coffins are hidden. The journey to a caring community where workers have a just wage with safe and dignified working conditions recalls the early labor vision that "an injury to one is an injury to all," which to people of faith sounds strangely similar to "Do unto others as you would have them do unto you."

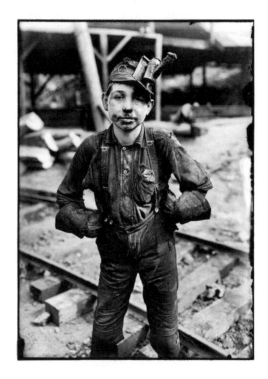

Photograph by Lewis Wickes Hine, 1908

Eleven year old "Tipple boy"
Macdonald, West Virginia

# WHEN MINERS MARCH - *A Review*
By Theresa Burriss Ph.D.

Theresa Burriss is Director of Appalachian Studies at Radford University. This review was first published in *APPALACHIAN HERITAGE.*

William C. Blizzard. *When Miners March.* Oakland, Calif.: PM Press, 2010. Wess Harris, ed. 407 pages with photos and appendices. Trade paperback, $21.95.

The recording and telling of history have proven to be troublesome for the critically-minded as inconsistencies, innocent mistakes, and downright lies plague much of what readers are given as purported fact. Of course as many realize, the "winners" or those in power have traditionally written history and delivered it in a neat, seemingly indisputable package. Fortunately, honest historians do exist and attempt to convey more accurate pictures of historical events, often working from a grassroots or "in the trenches" perspective that provides room for the typically forgotten or intentionally overlooked players.

William C. Blizzard offers readers just such a retelling of history that gets at the truth of the labor struggles leading up to the 1921 Battle of Blair Mountain in West Virginia. His work, *When Miners March*, first titled *Struggle and Lose...Struggle and Win!*, is well-researched and documented, offering court transcripts, newspaper articles, letters and written testimony from key players in the coalminers' efforts to unionize West Virginia.

The acquisition of the primary documents is due to William C. Blizzard's familial association with the labor fight, namely his father Bill Blizzard's role as a union

165

organizer beginning as early as the Paint and Cabin Creek skirmishes in 1912-13.

Offering a comprehensive history of coal in West Virginia, Blizzard starts his work in 1817 with the discovery of coal in the Kanawha Valley and then methodically moves forward, documenting the trials and tribulations of the miners in a year-by-year timeline. He even offers an historical interlude with primary accounts of the Ludlow, Colorado, massacre, where women and children, in addition to miners, were killed indiscriminately.

With Blizzard's meticulous attention to detail, readers come to appreciate the decade's long oppression exerted by the coal companies and understand how many local law enforcement agencies did the dirty bidding of those companies because they were paid handsomely to do so. Sheriff Don Chafin of Logan County is the most cited due to his ongoing ruthless oppression and often times outright murder of miners and their families.

Even West Virginia's governors were not above bribery and openly worked to suppress the miners through policy and legislation, both at the state and federal levels, more often than not resorting to lies about the miners and their tactics to justify such suppression.

In the telling Blizzard also disputes many formerly accepted "truths" about the labor movement. For example, several other historians have placed C. Frank Keeney, UMWA District 17 President, and Fred Mooney, District 17 Secretary-Treasurer, in the middle of the Battle of Blair Mountain, leading the charge instead of

Bill Blizzard, Sr. As son William Blizzard documents, however, the two union leaders were far removed from the site because of fears that they would fall to the same fate as Sid Hatfield and Ed Chambers, who'd been murdered in broad daylight by Baldwin-Felts "detectives" or gun thugs on the steps of the McDowell County Courthouse. No one was ever brought to trial over these murders. William Petry, a UMWA organizer, explains, "Keeney and Mooney disappeared. Where they are I don't know, but I'm assured they are safe from the hired gunmen at present" (p. 308).

I must say that it helps to have a general understanding of the history of coal and labor in Appalachia before diving into this work. In fact, when teaching this work in college classes, I found my students responded to it much better after they read Denise Giardina's historical fiction on the subject, *Storming Heaven*, and Diane Gilliam's poetry companion, *Kettle Bottom*. The novel and poetry provided an entrée into the grittier details of *When Miners March*. My students noted that it's easy to get lost in the dates and lose track of the names without having a previous understanding, and even so, they needed to process everything in class to fully grasp the import of Blizzard's work. The history made a lasting impression on my students, however, when they visited many of the sites where the miners fought, set up tent colonies, and were buried. This experiential fieldtrip offered a holistic education for my students and I highly recommend it to fellow educators. Indeed, Blizzard's work came to life as the students made connections between all those historical details and the tangible evidence before them.

For the scholar and labor historian, *When Miners March* provides incredible insight into one of the most tumultuous times in our nation's labor history. For anyone who participates in any kind of labor force, the work illustrates how much we owe to the coalminers of Appalachia who lived, and often times died, to secure basic freedoms and rights for all workers in the United States.

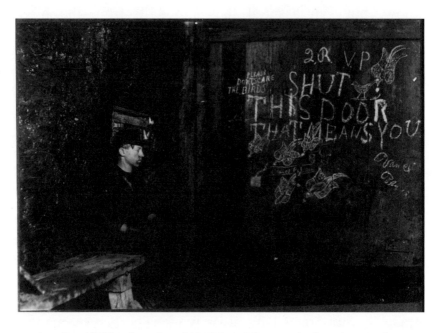

   In 1908 when Lewis Wickes Hine took the above photo, he noted that Vance, a 15 year old "trapper boy," had trapped for several years in that extremely dark WV Coal mine at $.75 a day for 10 hours of work. Hine also noted "All he does is to open and shut this door: most of the time he sits here idle, waiting for the cars to come."

   Vance would have been around 28 years old when miners marched to liberate WV's southern coal fields.

Still Marching.


MONTANI SEMPER LIBERI

# When Miners March

By William C. Blizzard
Edited by Wess Harris

---

### AN INSIDER'S LOOK AT THE LARGEST OPEN AND ARMED REBELLION IN U.S. HISTORY

---

$21.95 • 978-1-60486-300-0 • PAPERBACK •
6x9 • 408 PAGES • LABOR/ HISTORY-U.S.

The uprisings of coal miners that defined the Mine Wars of the 1920s were a direct result of the Draconian rule of the coal companies. The climax was the Battle of Blair Mountain, the largest open and armed rebellion in U.S. history. The Battle, and Union leader Bill Blizzard's quest for justice, was only quelled when the U.S. Army brought guns, poison gas, and aerial bombers to stop the 10,000 bandanna-clad miners who formed the spontaneous "Red Neck Army."

Over half a century ago, William C. Blizzard wrote the definitive insider's history of the Mine Wars and the resulting trial for treason of his father, the fearless leader of the Red Neck Army. This is a people's history, complete with previously unpublished family photos and documents. If it brawls a little, and brags a little, and is angry more than a little, well, the people in this book were that way.

## "An extraordinary account of a largely ignored but important event in the history of our nation."

—Howard Zinn, author of *A People's History of the United States*